BTEC First
Certificate in Applied Science

Knowledge Book

edexcel
advancing learning, changing lives

BTEC First
Certificate in Applied Science
Knowledge Book

Writing, editing and production

The **4science** team and associates

*www.***4science**.*org.uk*

Images

Photos.com [Jupiter Images]
(unless otherwise stated)

Publisher

Edexcel
190 High Holborn
London WC1V 7BH
United Kingdom

Copyright

© 2006 Edexcel Limited

All rights reserved.

No part of this publication may be reproduced, stored in a retrieval system or transmitted in any form or by any means, electronic, mechanical, photocopying, recording or otherwise without either the prior written permission of the publishers or a licence permitting restricted copying in the United Kingdom issued by the Copyright Licensing Agency Limited, 90 Tottenham Court Road, London W1P 9HE.

Seventh impression 2009

Printed in the United Kingdom

Safety

Teachers should make sure a risk assessment is carried out by a suitably qualified person before students undertake any practical activities.

A catalogue record for this book is available from the British Library
ISBN 1-84690-002-6

Letter from Edexcel

Welcome to the BTEC First Certificate in Applied Science *Knowledge Book*.

This book has some essential information that you can consult to help you complete your assignments and gain an understanding of relevant scientific topics you need to cover in your studies.

Every time you see words *in this colour and style* it means there's something to do. There are lots of questions to check what you know. You'll find diagrams to label and tables to complete as well as word searches, crosswords and other puzzles. Oh and before you panic we've provided answers so your can see that you've got them right. Did you know that using highlighter, making notes and reading out loud aids your memory too?

It is important for you to be able to organise and build up your portfolio of evidence for each unit to enable you to successfully complete the BTEC course. We have given you some tips about portfolio building.

To complete your portfolio of evidence for each unit you will be given a number of assignments that will count towards your final unit and course grade. Each of these assignments will have a deadline when you need to hand them in for marking.

We have provided a table for you to fill in with your assignment deadlines to help you remember when to hand in your coursework. There is also a progress sheet to enable you to keep a record of your progress throughout the course.

Of course, the *Knowledge Book* can't do everything for you. You still need to work hard to complete your coursework assignments and this will mean finding information from other sources.

Good Luck!

Contents page

	Introduction	3
	Assessment Evidence Grids (Units 3, 4 and 5)	4
	Portfolio guidance	7
	Example deadline table and progress report	8
	Deadline table and Progress record	9

Chemistry applications

Raw materials	10
Classifying chemicals	12
Atomic structure	14
Chemical bonding	16
Comparing materials	18
Properties and structure	20
Formulae and equations	22
Reacting masses	24
Chemical change	26
Getting metals from ores	28
Organic compounds	30
Our changing planet	32

Physical science applications

Conservation of energy	34
Energy loss and heat transfer	36
Conduction, convection and radiation	38
Radiation and waves part 1	40
Radiation and waves part 2	42
Fossil fuels	44
Alternative energy resources	46
Generating electricity	48
Choosing and using energy resources	50
Counting the cost	52
The Universe part 1	54
The Universe part 2	56
Sustainable Earth	58

Biological systems

Useful products from living organisms	60
Ecosystems	62
Farming	64
How organisms grow	66
Micro-organisms	68
Cells and their contents	70
How cells divide	72
Passing on genes	74
Controlling gene inheritance	76
Heart and lungs	78
The body at work	80
Micro-organisms and disease	82

Answers to questions	84

Introduction

During your course induction period your course tutor will provide you with information (sometimes contained in a student course handbook) about such items as:

- assignment work
- assignment deadlines
- building coursework portfolios
- information gathering
- how you will be assessed
- practical work and Health & Safety in science laboratories.

The BTEC First Certificate in Applied Science course you are studying is made up of three units:

Unit 3: Chemistry Applications

Unit 4: Physical Science Applications

Unit 5: Biological Systems.

These three units also form part of the Edexcel Level 2 BTEC First Diploma in Applied Science and therefore the information in this knowledge book is useful to you if you are studying this course.

BTEC courses are known as work-related courses and therefore the assignments you need to complete will have a work-related scenario e.g. testing the quality of river water for pollutants as an environmental scientist.

Your assignments will usually be broken down into a number of tasks that you will be asked to complete and can be similar to the tasks that you would do if you were working in that job role e.g. testing the river water to see if there is too much fertiliser in it which has come from nearby farms.

The BTEC First course that you are studying on has both course and unit grades.

You can achieve a pass, merit or distinction for a unit and for the overall course.

On successful completion, the certificate you receive will contain both the unit and course grades.

An example:

The individual units have the following grades	
Unit 3: Chemistry Applications	Pass
Unit 4: Physical Science Applications	Merit
Unit 5: Biological Systems	Merit
The overall grade for the BTEC First Certificate in Applied Science course would be - Merit	

You can track your progress by use of the Record of Progress table on page 9.

The *Assessment Evidence Grids* show the 18 items that your portfolio must contain to achieve a pass grade.

The grids also show the additional work that you need to include in your portfolio to achieve a merit grade or distinction grade.

Assessment Evidence Grid: Unit 3 Chemistry Applications

In order to pass this unit, the evidence that the learner presents for assessment needs to demonstrate that they can meet all of the learning outcomes for the unit. The criteria for a pass grade describe the level of achievement required to pass this unit.

To achieve a pass grade the evidence must show that the learner is able to:	To achieve a merit grade the evidence must show that, in addition to the pass criteria, the learner is able to:	To achieve a distinction grade the evidence must show that, in addition to the pass and merit criteria, the learner is able to:
P1 describe atomic and electronic structures of elements 1-20, including isotopes, in the periodic table	M1 describe the patterns and trends of chemical properties of groups 1 and 7 in the periodic table	D1 explain the patterns and trends within groups 1 and 7 in the periodic table
P2 investigate and describe ionic, covalent and metallic bonds	M2 investigate and explain the difference in properties of substances with ionic, covalent and metallic bonded substances	D2 explain bonding in terms of stability - a means of achieving a full outer shell either by transferring or sharing electrons
P3 carry out investigations to collect primary data to define what is meant by exothermic and endothermic reactions	M3 using examples of suitable investigations collect primary data and describe the differences between exothermic and endothermic reactions	D3 explain the processes involved in exothermic and endothermic reactions
P4 investigate and use primary data to identify the factors affecting reaction rates and reversible reactions	M4 investigate the use of primary data to describe how factors affect reaction rates and reversible reactions	D4 use primary data to evaluate how different factors affect reaction rates for a given industrial reaction
P5 investigate and describe the use of three main types of organic compounds used in society	M5 explain the benefits and disadvantages of using organic compounds in society	D5 evaluate the importance of organic compounds used in society
P6 describe how human and natural activities affect the earth and its environment.	M6 explain how human and natural activities affect the earth and its environment.	D6 evaluate the effects of human and natural activity on the earth and its environment.

Assessment Evidence Grid: Unit 4 Physical Science Applications

In order to pass this unit, the evidence that the learner presents for assessment needs to demonstrate that they can meet all of the learning outcomes for the unit. The criteria for a pass grade describe the level of achievement required to pass this unit.

To achieve a pass grade the evidence must show that the learner is able to:	To achieve a merit grade the evidence must show that, in addition to the pass criteria, the learner is able to:	To achieve a distinction grade the evidence must show that, in addition to the pass and merit criteria, the learner is able to:
P1 describe energy cycles in diagrams and in writing	M1 explain situations involving energy conversions and energy conservation within energy cycles	D1 calculate energy consumption and the efficiency of energy conversion in energy cycles
P2 list the different types of ionising radiations and their properties	M2 investigate the penetrating ability of different types of ionising radiation through different thickness of materials	D2 explain the reason for the different penetrating abilities of different types of ionising radiation through paper, aluminium and lead
P3 identify different types of waves and their main characteristics	M3 investigate different types of waves travelling in different materials (including a vacuum) and between different materials	D3 explain how waves may be used for communications
P4 describe two ways in which electricity may be produced	M4 explain two applications of electricity	D4 analyse the problem of energy losses when transmitting electricity and when converting it into other forms for consumer applications
P5 state methods used to investigate the universe, its galaxies, planets and stars.	M5 describe methods used to investigate the universe, its galaxies, planets and stars.	D5 analyse the effectiveness and limitations of methods used to investigate the universe, its galaxies, planets and stars.

Assessment Evidence Grid: Unit 5 Biological Systems

In order to pass this unit, the evidence that the learner presents for assessment needs to demonstrate that they can meet all of the learning outcomes for the unit. The criteria for a pass grade describe the level of achievement required to pass this unit.

To achieve a pass grade the evidence must show that the learner is able to:	To achieve a merit grade the evidence must show that, in addition to the pass criteria, the learner is able to:	To achieve a distinction grade the evidence must show that, in addition to the pass and merit criteria, the learner is able to:
P1 construct simple identification keys and describe the main characteristics within the major classification groups	M1 explain the need to classify organisms	D1 discuss the characteristics which are used to distinguish the major groups
P2 describe an ecosystem investigated and indicate the types of interdependence of living things in it	M2 describe examples of adaptations to the environment shown by organisms within the ecosystem	D2 construct quantitative and qualitative diagrams to demonstrate the relationships between organisms living interdependently within an ecosystem
P3 describe the possible effect of human activities on the ecosystem investigated	M3 describe the effect of these environmental changes over time and the means of measuring them	D3 analyse data relating to changes in the environment and explain how the environmental impact might be minimised in future
P4 describe the relationship between chromosomes, DNA and genes	M4 describe (using examples) how variation within a species brings about evolutionary change	D4 explain how genes control variation within a species using a simple coded message
P5 identify and describe two examples of inherited conditions and diseases	M5 identify the mechanisms by which these conditions and diseases are inherited	D5 investigate and describe the effectiveness of gene therapy to prevent inherited conditions and diseases
P6 describe the effects of four different factors which have a detrimental effect on human health	M6 explain the mechanisms involved in disrupting body systems, for each of the examples chosen	D6 describe the social issues which arise from each of the conditions described
P7 describe two control mechanisms which enable the human body to maintain optimum health.	M7 describe the differences between the actions of chemical and electrical protective mechanisms of the body.	D7 explain the effects of the chemical and hormonal controls on human health

Portfolio guidance

Your assignments should be stored in a portfolio. At the end of the course, the External Verifier from Edexcel will ask your teacher for particular samples of portfolio work. So, you must keep your portfolio well organised and safe.

What's in your portfolio?

Your assignments show how good you are at various scientific skills. The awarding body uses your assessment grades to calculate your overall course grade.

The board needs **evidence** that the marks awarded match the quality of work. It will check samples from some students in each school or college. They might choose **you**, so your portfolio needs to be complete.

Whose work?

The contents of your portfolio must be your own work.

- Be prepared to prove it to your teacher.
- Practical reports should include signed statements (*witness testimonies*), where relevant, from your teacher, stating:
  - you successfully carried out the procedure yourself
  - how much help you needed, if any.
- When you work as a team, each person must contribute. As a team member you yourself must:
  - do what the assessment criteria require
  - show your teacher that you've done so.
- **Note:** putting Internet or CD-ROM material straight into your portfolio does **not** count as your own work. You must show that you have **used** it by, for instance:
  - extracting the information you need for the assignment
  - rejecting all irrelevant material
  - combining information from several sources, and rewriting it in your own words.

Normally, your assignment brief will have a frontsheet. Make sure you have signed the sheet before you hand in your work.

Improving your grade

- Look at the Assessment Evidence grid for each unit. They show what you need to do for each grade.
- Before you submit an assignment for marking, check that you have done what the grid says, as well as you can.
- Ask your teacher to explain the criteria in more detail.

e-Portfolios

If you word-process your assignments you can store your portfolio electronically, including digital photographs etc. You will need to print out anything the awarding body asks to see.

In later years, after e-portfolio trials, the Verifier may access your portfolio online. Your index then becomes even more important, so that the Verifier can find particular pieces of evidence. (Note: you can still use a paper-based portfolio if you wish.)

Getting organised

Your portfolio should contain **all of your assessed work**.

- Keep all of your work in a portfolio.
- Make sure you highlight those items used for assessment.
- Towards the end of the course you should have your assignments ready for verification.

Organise your portfolio so that it's easy to find any item that the External Verifier asks to see.

- You could file assignments in the order given for each unit.
- Filing in date order, or just inserting new assignments at the front or back, may make it difficult to find particular items later.
- Use file separators or stick-on tabs between items.

Make an index to help find items later.

- Some assignments may cover more than one topic in a unit.
- In the index, list the assignments shown in the table, and say which assignment provides the evidence for each.

Make sure your name is on each page.

- Remember, it may be looked at by the External Verifier, who will not recognise your writing.

Number the pages within each assignment.

- They could get separated or dropped and scattered.

7

During your BTEC course you will be given a number of assignments for each unit. Each assignment will have a deadline of when you will need to hand them in to your unit teacher. Keeping a record of deadlines of your BTEC course assignments should help you organise and manage your workload.

Example deadline table

The table below shows you an example of a student who has started to fill in their unit assignment deadlines for the first year of a two year BTEC First Certificate in Applied Science course.

Learner Name: _Trevor Sanderson_   Course Leader: _S. Bhattacharya_

Unit	Assignment number	\multicolumn{11}{c}{Deadline for assignments during year 2006/7}
		Sep	Oct	Nov	Dec	Jan	Feb	Mar	Apr	May	Jun	Jul
3	1		12th									
3	2			23rd								
3	3					19th						
3	4							9th				
3	5									4th		
4	1			6th								
4	2						6th					
4	3								11th			

Example progress record

The table below shows you how to complete your record of progress. You can keep a record of your progress by ticking each individual unit grading criteria that you have completed in your assignment work. The example shows a learner's record of progress where they have completed two assignments, one for Unit 3 and one for Unit 4. They have not completed any assignments for Unit 5. In Assignment 1 for Unit 3, they achieved a pass for the grading criteria P1, a merit for the grading criteria M1 and distinction for the grading criteria D1. In Assignment 2 for Unit 4, they achieved a pass for the grading criteria P1 and P2, and a merit for grading criteria M1 and M2.

Assignment	Unit 3 P 1 2 3 4 5 6	Unit 3 M 1 2 3 4 5 6	Unit 3 D 1 2 3 4 5 6	Unit 4 P 1 2 3 4 5	Unit 4 M 1 2 3 4 5	Unit 4 D 1 2 3 4 5	Unit 5 P 1 2 3 4 5 6 7	Unit 5 M 1 2 3 4 5 6 7	Unit 5 D 1 2 3 4 5 6 7
1	X	X	X						
2				XX	XX				

8

Deadline table & Progress record

Learner Name: _____   Course Leader: _____

Deadline for assignments during year one

Unit	Assignment number	Sep	Oct	Nov	Dec	Jan	Feb	Mar	Apr	May	Jun	Jul

Deadline for assignments during year two

Unit	Assignment number	Sep	Oct	Nov	Dec	Jan	Feb	Mar	Apr	May	Jun	Jul

Assignment	Unit 3				Unit 4				Unit 5			
	P	M	D	P	M	D	P	M	D
	1 2 3 4 5 6	1 2 3 4 5 6	1 2 3 4 5 6	1 2 3 4 5	1 2 3 4 5	1 2 3 4 5	1 2 3 4 5 6 7	1 2 3 4 5 6 7	1 2 3 4 5 6 7

If you need to, photocopy this grid to add more assignments

Chemistry applications

Raw materials

The Earth provides us with the raw materials from which we can make a vast number of useful products, from building materials to medicines.
The way we extract and process these materials must be managed carefully.

Extracting raw materials

Raw materials are substances used as starting materials for making other substances. The main methods of getting them out of the ground are …

Quarrying
Examples: limestone, marble, granite.

Mining
Examples: gold, metal ores, rock salt.

Liquid mining
Liquid mining turns the solid mineral into a liquid before pumping it to the surface. For example, sulfur (by melting it); salt (by dissolving it in water to form brine - solution mining).

Drilling a well
For example: petroleum (crude oil).

Fill in the missing word
Solution mining is an example of _ _ _ _ _ _ _ mining.

Use or separate?

Some materials from the ground are used as they are. Others need separating and purifying before being used.

Used as they are:	What for?
limestone	buildings, roads, cement and chemicals
marble and granite	buildings
gold	jewellery and wiring computer chips
metal ores	making metals
rock salt	icy roads
sulfur	making sulfuric acid and rubber

Need separating:	Why?
rock salt	to get pure salt
crude oil	to separate fractions for different uses

Question 1
Why isn't rock salt purified before spreading on icy roads?

Answer

Getting pure salt from rock salt

Instead of digging out the rock salt:
- Pump water into rock salt underground. Salt dissolves. Clay and rocky impurities don't.
- Pump the salt solution (brine) up to the surface. This is solution mining.
- Boil the brine to evaporate the water. Pure salt crystallises out. Impurities stay dissolved.

The main separation occurs underground. Solution mining brings up only brine. The unwanted, insoluble impurities in the rock salt are left behind. Pure salt is obtained by evaporation of brine.

Question 2
Salt manufacturers use 'multiple effect evaporation' - steam from one evaporator heats the next, at lower pressure. Suggest one advantage of this method.

Answer

Separating oil fractions

Crude oil is a mixture of hundreds of compounds, mainly **hydrocarbons**. **Fractional distillation** separates these into groups (**fractions**), according to boiling point.

- Crude oil is heated to about 350 °C. Most of it vaporises (becomes a **vapour**). The compounds with boiling points above 350 °C remain liquid.
- Vapours and liquids pass into a **fractionating column**.
- Vapours rise up the column. Liquids (boiling points above 350 °C) flow down the column.
- Vapours in the column **condense to liquids** as they rise and cool.
- Different liquids (each still a mixture) condense at different heights. The lower the boiling point, the higher up the column they condense.

From air and sea

Air is a mixture of oxygen and nitrogen, with small amounts of other gases such as carbon dioxide. It's liquified under pressure at low temperatures. Oxygen and nitrogen are obtained by fractional distillation of liquid air. The principle is the same as separating oil fractions, but the temperatures are much lower:

boiling point of oxygen = –183 °C
boiling point of nitrogen = –196 °C

Oxygen is used for oxy-acetylene welding, as a respiratory aid for patients and in a number of industrial manufacturing processes.

The major use of nitrogen is for making ammonia in the Haber process. It's also used when an inert atmosphere is needed and as a refrigerant.

Question 4
What other gas is needed to make ammonia?

Answer

Sodium chloride is extracted from seawater in some places. For example: France, Slovenia and North Wales. Seawater also provides us with iodine.

Question 5
How is sodium chloride obtained from sea water?

Answer

Extract the raw materials from the jumbled letters ...

1. ETNESMOIL _____
2. CORK LAST _____ _____
3. DUREC LOI _____ _____
4. LUUFSR _____
5. TAMLE SREO _____ _____
6. RAMBEL _____

Separating oil fractions (continued ...)

Fractions are not used directly. Further processes convert them into useful products. For example:

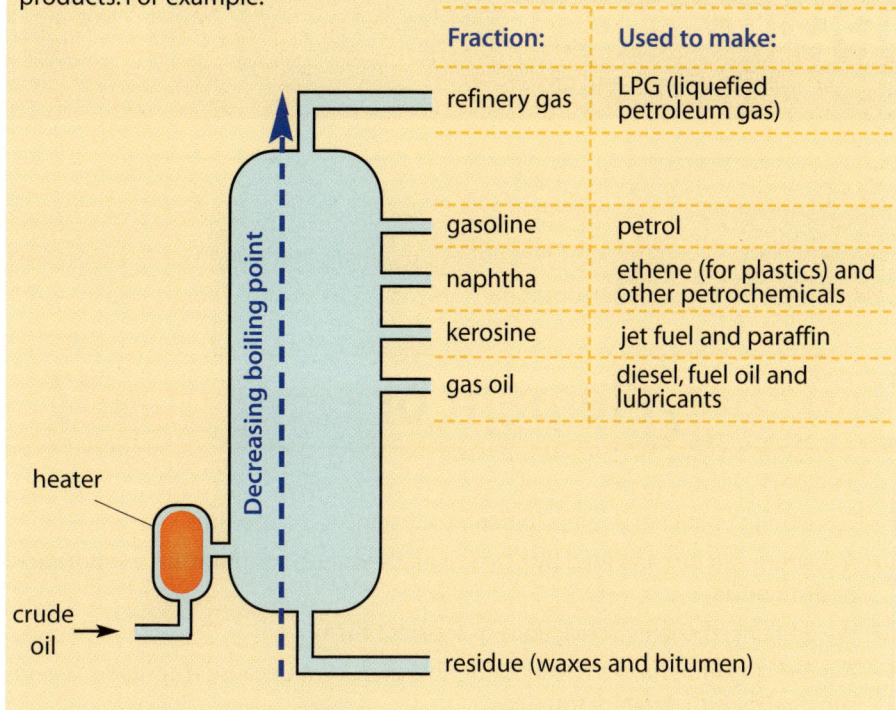

Fraction:	Used to make:
refinery gas	LPG (liquefied petroleum gas)
gasoline	petrol
naphtha	ethene (for plastics) and other petrochemicals
kerosine	jet fuel and paraffin
gas oil	diesel, fuel oil and lubricants
residue	(waxes and bitumen)

Decreasing boiling point

heater
crude oil

Try covering the labels to see how many you can remember.

Cracking the crude oil problem

The problem: Crude oils vary. However, all give too much of the high boiling point fractions and not enough gasoline.

The solution: The high boiling point fractions are 'cracked' to produce more of the substances needed to make petrol, plastics and other petrochemicals.

Question 3 (cover the diagram, above, before answering this)
(a) What are hydrocarbons?
(b) Which oil fraction is used to make petrol?
(c) Name one other oil fraction, and give one of its major uses.
(d) Which fraction from the column has the highest boiling point?

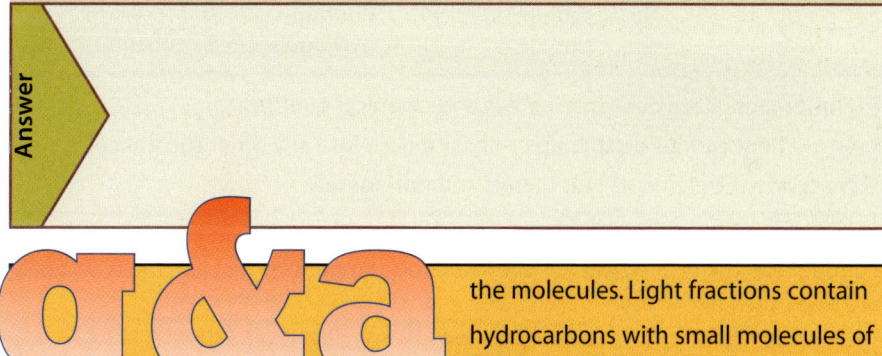

Answer

q & a

Q. What is meant by 'cracking' substances obtained from oil?
A. Heating the substances in order to break down large molecules into smaller ones.

Q. What is meant by 'light' and 'heavy' fractions?
A. These refer to the size and mass of the molecules. Light fractions contain hydrocarbons with small molecules of low mass. For example, hexane, C_6H_{14}. Heavy fractions contain much larger molecules. For example, eicosane, $C_{20}H_{42}$. Heavy fractions have higher boiling points than lighter fractions.

Q. What's the difference between kerosine and kerosene?
A. None, except the spelling.

Chemistry applications ▶▶▶▶ | Classifying chemicals

Chemical substances may be elements or compounds. Frequently they are found mixed together (mixtures). Elements may be described as metals or non-metals. Compounds may be described as organic or inorganic. Depending on the scale on which they are made, we classify chemical substances as bulk chemicals or fine chemicals.

Mixture, element or compound?

Mixtures
- Something containing several different substances is a **mixture**.
- A mixture can be separated by physical methods, such as **filtration**, **evaporation** or **distillation**.
- We don't need chemical reactions to separate them.
- A mixture cannot have a chemical formula of its own because it contains several substances with different formulae.

Mixture	Components
rock salt	sodium chloride, clay and various impurities
granite	speckled grains of various minerals
crude oil	many different hydrocarbons
brine	sodium chloride dissolved in water
air	nitrogen, oxygen and other gases

A pure material contains only one substance. It may be an **element** or a **compound**.

Elements
- There are about 100 elements. You need to know names and symbols for these 20.

Metals				Non-metals			
Al	aluminium	Mg	magnesium	Br	bromine	N	nitrogen
Ba	barium	K	potassium	C	carbon	O	oxygen
Ca	calcium	Ag	silver	Cl	chlorine	P	phosphorus
Fe	iron	Na	sodium	F	fluorine	Si	silicon
Pb	lead	Zn	zinc	H	hydrogen	S	sulfur

- All **elements** have one-word names and chemical symbols.
- An element **cannot** be split up or decomposed into any other substances.
- We divide the elements into **metals** and **non-metals**:

Metals ...	Non-metals ...
conduct electricity and heat	are insulators (do not conduct electricity or heat)
are silver-grey and shiny	
have a high density	have low density (less than 3 g/cm³)
bend without breaking	are gases brittle solids (bromine is a liquid)

Compounds
- Most pure substances are **compounds**. There are millions of different ones.
- If the name or chemical formula includes two or more elements (for example, iron oxide, Fe_2O_3, or calcium carbonate, $CaCO_3$), the material is a compound. However, many compounds have one-word names such as water or methane.
- A compound can be decomposed or changed into other chemicals - but only by a chemical reaction.
- The products of the reaction may be elements or other compounds.

Formulating mixtures

Scientists spend a lot of time separating mixtures to obtain elements or compounds. For example, they obtain sodium chloride from rock salt and hydrocarbons from crude oil. You can read about this in *Raw materials*.

Chemical reactions usually produce mixtures. Scientists separate these to obtain the elements or compounds that are produced. Separation science is important.

Having taken the trouble to separate pure elements or compounds, chemists frequently mix them up again! But it's not a haphazard process. Nearly all the products you buy in shops, pharmacies, supermarkets, garden centres and DIY stores are mixtures. Medicines, cosmetics, perfumes, washing powders and liquids, and fertilisers are examples.

Formulation chemists work out the best combination of ingredients. The combination usually includes active ingredients and non-active ingredients.

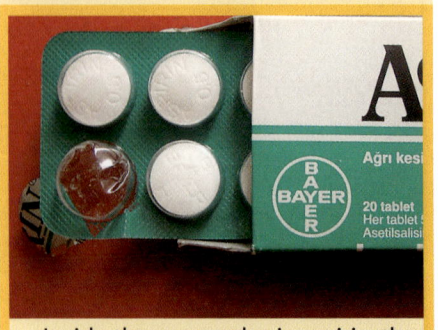

Inside these capsules is aspirin, the active ingredient. The capsule is made of non-active ingredients.

Question 1
Name the elements in each of the following compounds:
(a) NaBr (b) CaF$_2$ (c) SiO$_2$ (d) PCl$_3$ (e) AgNO$_3$ (f) PbSO$_4$

Organic and inorganic compounds

Organic means **from organisms**. Some organic compounds, like sugar, are extracted from plants, animals or micro-organisms. But most are made from chemicals obtained from petroleum, natural gas or coal - materials from organisms that lived long ago.

To decide whether a compound is organic or inorganic:

- Look for **C** (carbon) in the formula (not Ca, Cu, Cl, and so on).
- If the formula includes **C**, the compound is **organic** ...
  ... **except** for CO, CO$_2$ and metal carbonates (formulae with a CO$_3$ group. For example, Na$_2$CO$_3$).
- Any compound **without** C in its formula is **inorganic**.

Question 2
Which of the following are organic compounds?

A. C$_2$H$_4$ D. CH$_3$COOH
B. NaHCO$_3$ E. CO$_2$
C. C$_2$H$_5$OH   F. CuCO$_3$

Here are the formulae of some inorganic compounds. Complete the table by adding their names ...

Formula	Name	Formula	Name	Formula	Name
NH$_3$	_____	Fe$_2$O$_3$	**iron** _____	KNO$_3$	**potassium** _____
CO$_2$	**carbon** _____	PbO	_____	AgNO$_3$	_____
H$_2$O	_____	NaOH	_____ **hydroxide**	BaSO$_4$	_____ **sulfate**
HCl	_____ **acid**	BaCl$_2$	**barium** _____	CuSO$_4$	**copper** _____
H$_2$SO$_4$	**sulfuric** _____	NaCl	_____ **chloride**	Na$_2$SO$_4$	_____
CaO	_____ **oxide**	CaCO$_3$	**calcium** _____		
		CuCO$_3$	_____	... and this organic compound	
		Na$_2$CO$_3$	_____ **carbonate**	CH$_4$	_____

Bulk and fine chemicals

Bulk chemicals are made and used in large amounts - millions of tonnes per year.
- Each of them has a wide range of uses.
- Most of them are used in industry, mainly to make other chemicals.
- They are all sold in bulk, by the lorry-load or tanker-full.

Fine chemicals or **speciality chemicals** are made in smaller amounts, because much less is needed.
- Their uses are more limited - sometimes very specific (for only one purpose).
- Most are used on a small scale - often by the general public.
- Many are used as ingredients in other products, rather than sold separately.
- They are usually sold in small quantities - often in packets.

Remember these examples. Try drawing them or cutting pictures from magazines:

Bulk chemicals	Major uses
ammonia	fertilisers, nylon, nitric acid
chlorine	pvc, organic solvents, bleach
iron and steel	construction (for example, buildings and vehicles)
polyethene	packaging (for example, sheet and bottles), pipes
sulfuric acid	detergents, paints, other chemicals

Fine /speciality chemicals	Uses
medicines (pharmaceuticals)	each one is specific to a particular medical problem
dyes	specific for each colour and type of fabric
pigments	for paints and printing inks

Note: These are **types** of chemical, not **specific compounds**. There are many of each.

Question 3
Is each of the following a bulk or fine chemical, and is it organic or inorganic?

(a) sodium chloride - used to make many different chemicals, as well as food uses (b) indigo - makes jeans blue - can be extracted from a plant (c) titanium dioxide - makes brilliant white paint white (d) magnesium oxide - used in indigestion tablets (e) polystyrene - widely used plastic made from oil (f) aspirin - used as a pain reliever.

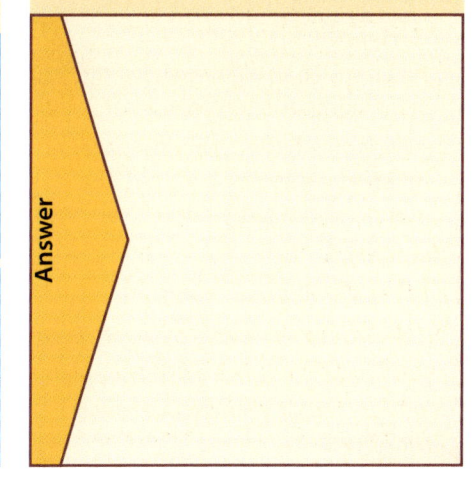

13

Chemistry applications

Atomic structure

Atoms are the basic building blocks of you and everything that surrounds you. They are made up of protons, neutrons and electrons.

Atoms: nature's building blocks

You are made up of atoms. So is everything around you - natural or man-made, visible or invisible (like air). Atoms make up everything except 'nothing'.

Question 1
Can you think of an example of 'nothing'?

Answer

Your body consists of many parts. Each part contains materials such as flesh and blood. The cells of each material contain millions of molecules of chemical compounds. Each molecule is made up of a group of atoms. Your body is built from about fifty million, million, million, million (5×10^{25}) atoms - a number far bigger than anybody can imagine!

Atomic number: an atom's ID

Every element has an **atomic number**, between 1 for hydrogen and 92 for uranium. The atomic number is the number of protons in the nucleus (also the total number of electrons). It's different for each element and is always a whole number.

- All atoms of an element have the same number of protons.
- Atoms of different elements have different numbers of protons. The atomic number identifies the element.

Question 3
Look at the diagram (right).
(a) How many protons in a carbon atom?
(b) How many electrons in a chlorine atom? (c) Which element has atoms with 7 protons?

What's in an atom?

Atoms are made up of even smaller particles. These are **protons**, **neutrons** and **electrons**. They are **sub-atomic** particles. You need to remember:
- the charge and mass of each;
- where they are in the atom;
- how to work out how many of each there are in an atom.

In diagrams, the electrons are shown in layers, called **shells**. These are like layers in an onion. The diagram shows a cross-section, like an onion cut in half.

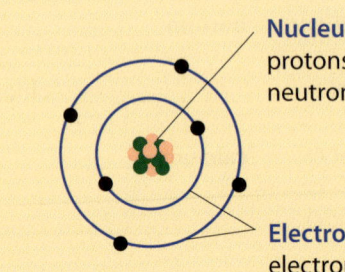

Nucleus. Contains protons ● and neutrons ●.

Electron shells. Contain electrons ●.

For any atom:
- number of protons = number of electrons
  so charges balance out, making the atom electrically neutral
- most of its mass is in its nucleus, since electrons have very little mass compared with protons and neutrons.

Question 2
Which sub-atomic particles have a negative charge, and which positive?

Answer

Part of a periodic table:

6	7	8	9	10
C	N	O	F	Ne
12.0	14.0	16.0	19.0	20.2
14	15	16	17	18
Si	P	S	Cl	Ar
28.1	31.0	32.0	35.5	39.9

Atomic number
Relative atomic mass

Answer

14

The periodic table

Elements are arranged in the periodic table in order of increasing atomic number.

The rows in the table are called **periods**.

As you look across the periodic table you'll see that the elements change character in a similar way in each period.

One trend is from metals to non-metals.

The columns in the table are called **groups**. They are numbered.

For example:

- The first column (beginning with lithium) is **group 1**. These elements are also known as the **alkali metals**.

- The seventh column (beginning with fluorine) is **group 7**. These elements are also known as the **halogens**.

- The eighth column (beginning with helium) is not called group 8. It's called **group 0**.

Elements in a group have similar chemical reactions to one another.

Question 4

(a) Name the elements in group 1 in order of increasing atomic number.

1 _____
2 _____
3 _____
4 _____
5 _____

(b) Name the elements in period 3 (the one that starts with sodium).

- _____
- _____
- _____
- _____
- _____
- _____

Atomic mass: counting p's and n's

All atoms are made from the same sub-atomic particles. A neutron (n^o) has the same mass as a proton (p^+). So we can compare masses of atoms by counting the numbers of protons and neutrons. For example:

- A hydrogen atom has only $1p^+$.
- An oxygen atom has $8p^+$ and $8n^o$.
- An oxygen atom is 16 times heavier than a hydrogen atom: its **mass number** = 16.

For any atom: **mass number = total number of protons and neutrons in its nucleus**.

Note: we ignore electrons, since even a hundred of them weigh less than one proton.

This is how we can write this information:

mass number ⟶ $^{12}_{6}C$ ⟵ symbol of the element
atomic number ⟶

Complete this table:

Number of p^+	Number of n^o	Number of e^-	Atomic number	Mass number
9	10	9	(a) _____	(b) _____
11	12	(c) _____	(d) _____	23
(e) _____	34	(f) _____	29	(g) _____
(h) _____	(i) _____	(j) _____	82	207

q & a

Q. What's the difference between 'mass number' and 'relative atomic mass'?

A. Some elements have atoms with different numbers of neutrons, so different mass numbers. For example, $^{35}_{17}Cl$ and $^{37}_{17}Cl$ have 18 and 20 neutrons respectively.

- Atoms of the same element with different mass numbers are called **isotopes**.
- The atomic number cannot change.

Relative atomic mass is the **average** mass of all the atoms of the element. For example:

- about 75% of chlorine atoms are $^{35}_{17}Cl$ and 25% are $^{37}_{17}Cl$
- the average mass is therefore about $(^{75}/_{100} \times 35) + (^{25}/_{100} \times 37) = 35.5$
- so, the relative atomic mass of chlorine is about 35.5.

Atomic fact file ...

Complete these six facts:

(a) atomic number = number of _____

(b) number of _____ = number of protons

(c) _____ = number of protons + number of neutrons

(d) number of _____ = mass number - number of protons

(e) _____ number = mass of one particular atom

(f) _____ atomic mass = average mass of all atoms of the element, including different isotopes.

15

Chemistry applications

Chemical bonding

Electrons are used to bond atoms together.
They may be shared by atoms (a covalent bond) or transferred from one atom to another (an ionic bond).

Electron shells

Electrons move in **shells** arranged around the nucleus of an atom (like layers in an onion). Each shell can hold more electrons than the one before.
- up to 2 in the 1st shell
- up to 8 in the 2nd
- up to 18 in the 3rd.

The **electron arrangement** can be shown by **diagrams** or **numbers**. For example:

Hydrogen (atomic number = 1)

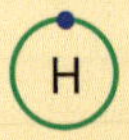

H   H 1

Carbon (atomic number = 6)

C   C 2.4

Sodium (atomic number = 11)

Na   Na 2.8.1

Question 1
What is the electron arrangement in:
(a) fluorine (Atomic number = 9)
(b) aluminium (Atomic number = 13)
(c) sulfur (Atomic number = 16)?

Answer

Important!

Although shown as • and x all electrons are the same. Using • and x lets you see where they started.

Ionic bonding: give-and-take

An **ion** forms when an atom or group of atoms loses or gains one or more electrons.
- Metal atoms form positive ions (**cations**) by passing electrons to non-metal atoms.
- Non-metals form negative ions (**anions**) by gaining electrons from metal atoms.

Neither can happen without the other. So, when a metal reacts with a non-metal, **both** positive and negative ions are formed. Since opposite charges attract, the ions bond to each other, forming a **lattice** of cations and anions. There are **no** individual molecules of ionic compounds.

An ionic bond is the electrostatic attraction between +ve and –ve ions. Only compounds containing metal **and** non-metal elements have ionic bonding.

Question 2
Why are metal ions positively charged?

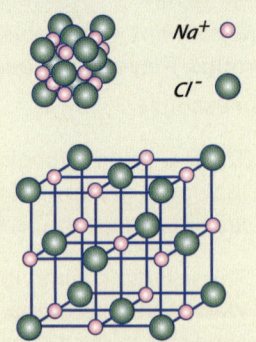

Answer

Part of the sodium chloride giant lattice.
The ions pack together closely (top picture). We use an exploded diagram (bottom picture) to make the positions of the ions easier to see.

Na⁺ ○
Cl⁻ ○

Electron transfer

Atoms with eight electrons in their outer shell, such as neon (2.8) or argon (2.8.8) are unreactive. When a metal reacts with a non-metal, both end up with this stable 'noble gas structure' of eight outer electrons.
- Metal atoms transfer outer electrons to non-metal atoms, leaving a shell of eight.
- Non-metal atoms **gain** electrons until their outer shell has eight.

For example:

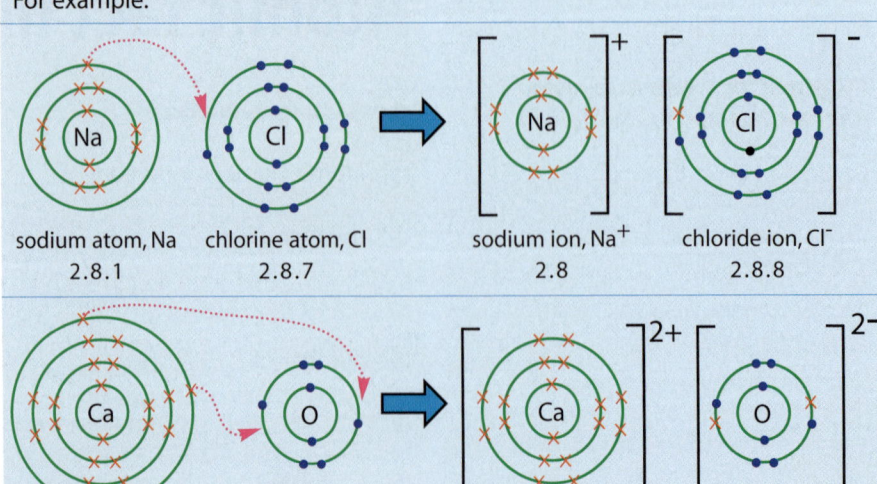

sodium atom, Na   chlorine atom, Cl   →   sodium ion, Na⁺   chloride ion, Cl⁻
2.8.1   2.8.7   2.8   2.8.8

calcium atom, Ca   oxygen atom, O   →   calcium ion, Ca²⁺   oxide ion, O²⁻
2.8.8.2   2.6   2.8.8   2.8

16

Electrons and reactivity

Group 1 elements have one electron in their outer shell. When they react, this electron is taken away, leaving an ion with a 1+ charge.

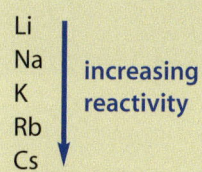

Li
Na
K   increasing
Rb   reactivity
Cs

Outer electron is taken away more easily because it's shielded from the attraction of the nucleus by inner shell electrons.

Result …
the reactivity of group 1 elements increases with increasing atomic number.

For example, group 1 elements react with water to give an alkaline solution. Reactivity increases down the group. Lithium reacts gently with water, but caesium reacts explosively.

Group 7 elements have seven electrons in their outer shell. When they react, an electron is gained producing an ion with a 1- charge.

F
Cl   decreasing
Br   reactivity
I

The electron is attracted more strongly when there are fewer inner shell electrons to shield it from the nucleus.

Result …
the reactivity of group 7 elements decreases with increasing atomic number.

For example, a group 7 element displaces another one lower in the group:

$Cl_2 + 2I^- \rightarrow 2Cl^- + I_2$

Question 5
Write an equation to show what happens when chlorine is bubbled through a solution of sodium bromide.

Question 3
(a) What is the charge and electron arrangement of (i) a potassium ion? (ii) a sulfide ion?
(b) Work out the formula for potassium sulfide.
(Note: Atomic number of K = 19, S = 16)

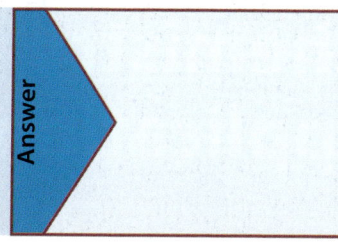

Covalent bonding: no charge for sharing

When non-metals react with each other they form **covalent** bonds, not ionic. The atoms share enough electrons to achieve the *noble gas structure*. For example:

Element	Number of electrons	Number shared	Total electrons	
H	1	1	2 (like He)	2
Cl	17	1	18 (like Ar)	2.8.8
O	8	2	10 (like Ne)	2.8
C	6	4	10 (like Ne)	2.8

One shared pair of electrons makes a covalent bond. The electrons attract the nuclei of both atoms, bonding them together. Two pairs shared by the same atoms make a **double bond**. You can show covalent bonding by drawing:

- *dot-and-cross* diagrams (outer shells only are shown)
- *displayed formulae*.

Covalent bonding usually produces **molecules** (individual groups of atoms). Unlike ions, molecules have no charge.

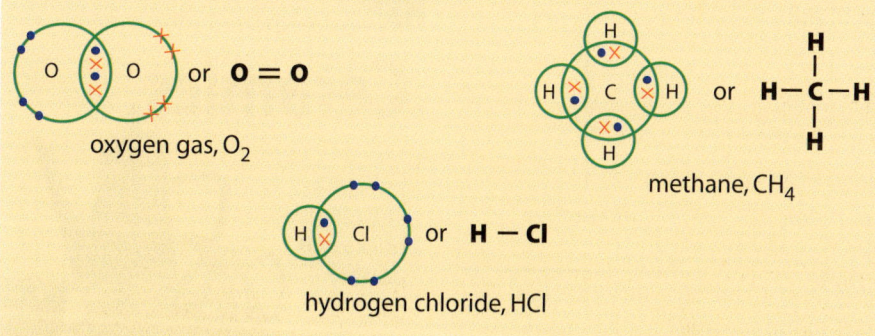

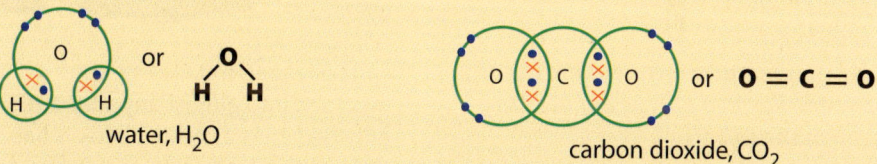

oxygen gas, O_2 — or $O=O$

methane, CH_4

hydrogen chloride, HCl — or $H-Cl$

water, H_2O

carbon dioxide, CO_2 — or $O=C=O$

Question 4
Which type of bonding does each of the following have?
(i) chlorine gas, Cl_2 (ii) potassium fluoride, KF (iii) ethanol, C_2H_5OH

Dative covalent bonds

Sometimes one atom provides both the electrons in a covalent bond. This is called a dative covalent bond. The bond is represented by → rather than —. Two examples:

ammonium ion, NH_4^+

carbon monoxide

17

Chemistry applications

Comparing materials

Most materials belong to one of the four families (or classes): **metals**, **polymers**, **ceramics**, **composites**. Each family has many members. All members in a family are different, but have similar properties.

Metals

This family contains pure metals and alloys.

Metals you need to know about

K	potassium	very reactive ↑
Na	sodium	
Ba	barium	
Ca	calcium	
Mg	magnesium	
Al	aluminium	
Zn	zinc	
Fe	iron	
Pb	lead	
Cu	copper	
Ag	silver	
Au	gold	unreactive

Two important alloys

Steel (iron + carbon + other metals)
Brass (copper + zinc)

Question 1
(a) Suggest why metals at the top of the list (K to Ca) are not used to make objects.
(b) Which other metal is added to steel to make stainless steel?

Answer

Polymers

A polymer is a huge molecule made up of the same group of atoms repeated over and over in long chains. Natural polymers include proteins, starch and DNA. However, polymers used to make things are mainly plastics (synthetic polymers) or rubber (natural or synthetic).

Some common plastic polymers

polyethene, polystyrene, polyvinylchloride (pvc), polyester, nylon, perspex

Question 2
(a) Name one other common plastic polymer.
(b) Why are most polymers named **poly-something**?

Answer

Ceramics

Ceramics include glass, bricks and pottery (such as china, porcelain and earthenware). Wet clay can be moulded into almost any shape. It only becomes a ceramic after it has dried and been heated to a very high temperature.

Question 3
Bricks and pottery are made by firing clay. How is clay fired?

Answer

Composites

Composites are made from two or more different materials combined together to give the best properties of each. They may consist of layers, or one material embedded in a matrix of another.

Some layered composites

- plywood (layers with grain in different directions)
- TetraPak™ carton (cardboard-aluminium-polyethene).

Some matrix composites

- reinforced concrete (steel rods in concrete)
- fibreglass (GRP) (glass fibres in polymer resin).

Question 4
Name one other fibre used in composites.

Answer

Natural vs synthetic

Everything starts as raw materials. We change many into man-made materials. Why? Because they are *better* in various ways. For example, in many applications: plastic polymers are preferred to wood; synthetic fibres have replaced wool, cotton and silk; brick has replaced stone. However, they also have some disadvantages. Think about what these might be.

New materials

Smart materials are unusual. Nitinol (a nickel and titanium alloy), for example, contracts when it's heated instead of expanding.

It's also a shape memory alloy. This means that if its shape changes, it returns to the original shape when heated or cooled.

Shape memory alloys are used in robotics, aircraft and surgery.

Thermochromic materials change colour when the temperature changes.

Photochromic materials change colour when light shines on them. For example, spectacle lenses can darken when you go from a dark room into bright sunshine.

Other smart materials include self-cleaning glass.

Many polymers have been designed to have special properties.

Some examples:

Kevlar
used in bullet-proof vests and helmets for Formula 1 drivers

Gortex™
a waterproof material that allows air to pass, keeping you dry but not sweaty

Lycra™
a stretchy, clingy material

Thinsulate™
a mixture of poly(propene) and polyester.

Find the four types of materials hidden here ...

A	S	P	B	K	Y
H	E	O	R	C	S
M	T	L	J	Q	C
M	I	Y	G	O	I
E	S	M	Y	I	M
T	O	E	L	X	A
A	P	R	V	H	R
L	M	S	I	K	E
S	O	R	X	S	C
J	C	D	A	B	M

Comparing properties

A material's properties are:
- similar to those of the same class (family)
- different from those of other classes.

Sometimes you can look at or feel materials when classifying them. When you can't look at or feel them, you have to use information from a database.

To select the best material for a particular purpose, you need to decide what properties are needed to do the job and match them to materials.

Below are the typical properties of the four classes. Use the empty boxes to give three examples of objects made from the different classes. But remember - you must be able to explain why the object is made from the particular material. Check your answers with your teacher.

Properties of metals

- High electrical and thermal conductivity - conduct electricity and heat well.
- Malleable - can be hammered, pressed or bent into shape, or rolled into sheets.
- Strong - can withstand heavy weights and forces without breaking.
- Hard (some are harder than others).
- Most metals have higher density than non-metals.
- Reactive metals corrode easily - they react with air and water (for example iron rusts).
- Unreactive metals resist corrosion.

Properties of plastic polymers

- Can be moulded into shape - **plastic** means mouldable, as in **plastic**ine.
- Low electrical and thermal conductivity - poor electrical and heat conductors, good electrical and heat insulators.
- Firm and rigid when moulded, but flexible when made as thin sheets or fibres (can be made more flexible by adding a plasticiser).
- Tough and strong for their mass - some are brittle.
- Low density - some less dense than water (< 1 g cm^{-3}).
- Not affected by air and water - many also resist acids, alkalis and solvents.

Thermoplastics	Thermosets
soften and melt on heating	set hard on heating (like an egg)
plastic is melted, then shaped in a mould	must be moulded while plastic is being made
can be recycled by softening and remoulding	cannot be melted, so not recyclable

Properties of ceramics

- Low electrical and thermal conductivity.
- Very high melting point.
- Very hard, but brittle.
- Resistant to air, water and chemicals.
- Glass is transparent.

Properties of composites

Composites combine the properties of their components. For example, reinforced concrete combines the **compressive strength of concrete** and the **tensile strength of steel**.

Some objects are made from more than one material. A saucepan has a metal base because it conducts heat and a plastic/wood handle because it doesn't. Try to think of three more examples - again, check your answers with your teacher.

Chemistry applications

Properties and structure

Materials used to make things are usually classified as metals, polymers, ceramics and composites.

Metallic bonding and structure: a sea of electrons

Metals lose their outer electrons to form positive metal ions. With no non-metal to gain them, the electrons stay attracted to the positive metal ions, but are free to move around between them. This produces a regular lattice of ions surrounded by a 'sea' of mobile electrons.

This structure explains the characteristic properties of metals.

- **Electrical conductivity:** electrons in the 'sea' are not attached to any particular ion. They can move. When a voltage is applied, the electrons flow, producing a current.
- **Malleability:** metals aren't brittle. They dent or bend when hit, because layers can slide over each other. They remain held together by the electrons.
- **High density and hardness:** most metals contribute several outer electrons per atom to the 'sea'. These hold the ions tightly. Although layers can move (by denting, bending or scratching) it takes a large force.
- **Metals are crystalline:** metal ions repel each other, so become evenly spaced, forming a regular lattice (see diagram).

Question 1
Suggest why sodium and potassium are softer and less dense than most other metals.

Answer

Alloying: disrupting the lattice

An alloy is made by mixing a metal with another substance. This might be another metal or a non-metal. The atoms of the substance might be bigger or smaller than those of the metal. Some alloys are made to make a metal stronger. Steel is an alloy of iron and carbon. It's stronger and less malleable than pure iron. Carbon atoms mixed into the iron lattice stop the layers sliding over one another as easily. Alloying may also lower the melting point. For example, solder, a lead/tin alloy, melts at a lower temperature than either lead or tin.

Question 2
(a) What metal is added to copper to make brass? (b) Is brass more or less malleable than pure copper? Why?

Answer

Structure of polymers: tangled chains

Polymer molecules are chains thousands of units long. Sometimes they simply lie side-by-side, but each molecule is flexible and often they get tangled together. The properties of polymers are due to these tangled chains.

- **Flexibility:** for a polymer to bend, its chains must slide past each other. The forces between one molecule and another depend on chemical structure. So some polymers are more flexible than others. Adding a plasticiser 'lubricates' the tangle by getting between the molecule chains. The chains slide more easily, increasing flexibility.
- **Hardness:** for the same reason, some polymers can be scratched and dented more easily than others.
- **Softening:** heating a **thermoplastic** makes the chains move more, and begin to flow. The polymer becomes softer, and easier to mould. On cooling they move less, and set in the moulded shape.
- **Melting:** polymer molecules have random lengths, so molecular mass varies. Therefore, a polymer has no definite melting point. Thermoplastics gradually soften over a range of temperature until completely molten. Increasing the average chain length increases the melting point, and improves mechanical strength.

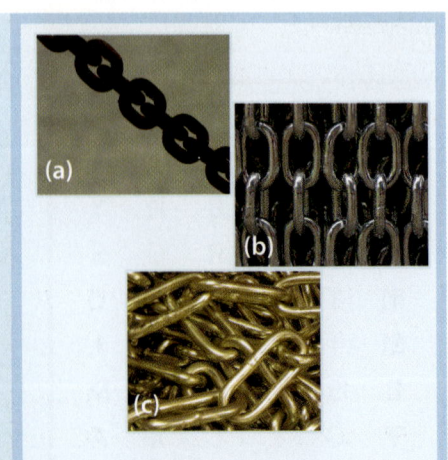

You can see these chains with the naked eye. But polymer molecule *chains* can't even be seen with a microscope! The images should help you to picture:
(a) a single polymer molecule;
(b) polymer molecules lying side-by-side;
(c) tangled polymer molecules.

20

Ionic bonding

Compounds with ionic bonding:
- are hard, brittle crystalline solids ... the ions are held together in giant lattices
- conduct electricity when molten ... the ions are free to move
- dissolve in water (not all of them) ... ions on the surface attract water molecules, become surrounded by them and float away exposing more ions - and so on.

Covalent bonding

Compounds with covalent bonding fall into two types:

1 molecular structures

Covalent bonds in molecules are strong, but bonding between one molecule and another is weak, e.g. water, ammonia, methane:
- have low melting and boiling points
- do no conduct electricity even when liquid
- dissolve in organic solvents, but not in water.

2 giant structures

Covalent bonding is equally strong throughout, e.g. silicon dioxide (sand):
- have high melting and boiling points
- do no conduct electricity even when liquid
- insoluble in most solvents.

Find the four hidden metals.
Pair them off to make two alloys and name the alloys ...

I	B	D	Y	B	D	G	R
Z	U	F	P	K	R	Q	D
N	I	Z	A	N	L	R	K
M	C	N	H	Z	E	D	Y
Z	W	H	C	P	A	H	C
N	G	U	P	E	T	I	N
T	C	O	L	P	R	H	P
H	C	J	K	X	H	D	K

---

q & a

Q. *Why do 'side groups' make polymers harder and less flexible?*

A. Side groups, such as -CH$_3$ in poly(propene) or -C$_6$H$_5$ in poly(styrene), stick out from the polymer chain. They interlock, making it more difficult for chains to slide past each other (see diagram, below).

Q. *Why don't thermoset plastics melt?*

A. When a thermoset polymer is made, **cross-links** (bonds) form between the chains, producing a rigid 3-dimensional network. The bonds don't break easily, the chains can't slide when heated, so the polymer can't become liquid.

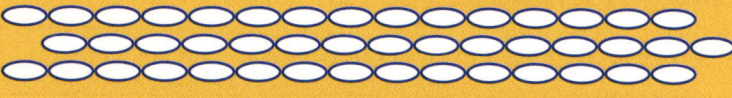

polymer chains without side groups slide past each other easily

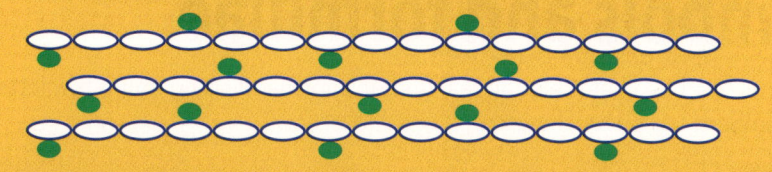

polymer chains with side groups interlock, making it difficult to slide past each other

---

Question 3
Why are light fittings made from a thermoset polymer, but wiring for the light is insulated with plasticised pvc?

Answer ▶

Ceramics: giant structures

Ceramics are solid inorganic substances. They only form at very high temperatures.

Aluminium oxide, Al$_2$O$_3$, and silicon dioxide (silica), SiO$_2$, are examples. Silicon carbide, SiC, is another.

Aluminium oxide and silica both have **giant structures**: every atom is bonded to several others around it in a giant lattice. Aluminium oxide has ionic bonds. Silica has covalent bonds.

Question 4: What type of bonds are in silicon carbide?

Answer ▶

Giant structures give ceramics characteristic properties.

- **Very high melting point:** much heat energy is needed to break all the bonds, before particles can separate and become liquid. Melting points are around 2000 °C.
- **Electrical and thermal insulation:** the electrons are fixed in bonds, not free to move, so no current can flow. Strong bonding also limits vibration, so the particles can't pass on heat energy easily.
- **Hard, but brittle:** the lattice doesn't let particles move. So, ceramics are difficult to dent or scratch, and aren't flexible. Force breaks the lattice apart.

Firing clay

Wet clay can be moulded because water between the layers of aluminosilicate (Al, Si and O) lets them slide around. Heating strongly in a kiln evaporates all the water and bonds form between the layers. So fired pottery is hard and rigid.

21

Chemistry applications

Formulae and equations

Chemists have their own shorthand for chemicals substances.
When chemical reactions occur, chemical substances (the reactants) are changed into different chemical substances (the products). Chemists use chemical equations to summarise these changes.

Symbols and formulae

Scientists describe chemicals and reactions in shorthand, using only a few letters and numbers.

Symbols
- Every element has its own symbol.
- When the symbol has two letters the second letter must be lower case (such as Na, *not* NA).

Formulae
- A chemical formula shows which elements the compound contains, and the ratio of atoms of each element. For example:
  Fe_2O_3 is made up of iron (Fe) atoms and oxygen (O) atoms.
  The ratio of atoms is 2:3 (Fe_2O_3).
  Na_2CO_3 is made up of sodium (Na) atoms, carbon (C) atoms and oxygen (O) atoms. The ratio of atoms is 2:1:3 (Na_2CO_3).
- Many metal compounds contain groups of non-metals with the same name and formula. For example: carbonate -CO_3, nitrate -NO_3 and sulfate -SO_4.

Word equations

Word equations tell you, in words, the reactants and products of a chemical equation. There is always an arrow in between. For example, the word equation for burning methane is:

methane + oxygen → carbon dioxide + water
reactants — read as "react together to make" — products

The **reactants** react with each other and are changed into the **products**.

Question 1
(a) Which elements does copper sulfate ($CuSO_4$) contain, and what is the ratio of atoms?
(b) Use the tables of symbols and formulae (on page 28-29) to work out the names of these compounds: (i) KCl (ii) $PbSO_4$ (iii) $MgCO_3$ (iv) SO_2

Answer

Note: if there's only one atom of an element, no number is shown. For example, copper sulfate is written $CuSO_4$ **not** $Cu_1S_1O_4$

Chemical reactions

Chemists classify different types of chemical reaction. For example:

Neutralisation
When an acid reacts with a base to make a salt and water only, e.g:
word equation:
sodium hydroxide + hydrochloric acid → sodium chloride + water
chemical equation:
$NaOH + HCl \rightarrow NaCl + H_2O$

Hydration and dehydration
Hydration is when water reacts with a substance, e.g:
word equation:
ethene + water → ethanol
chemical equation:
$C_2H_4 + H_2O \rightarrow C_2H_5OH$
Note: this is not the same as something dissolving in water
Dehydration is the opposite, e.g:
word equation:
ethanol → ethene + water
chemical equation:
$C_2H_5OH \rightarrow C_2H_4 + H_2O$

Oxidation and reduction
Oxidation is gain of oxygen and reduction is loss of oxygen, e.g:
word equation:
copper oxide + carbon → copper + carbon dioxide
chemical equation:
$2CuO + 2C \rightarrow Cu + CO_2$
Copper oxide is reduced and carbon is oxidised.
Oxidation is also defined as loss of electrons, and reduction as gain of electrons. This may help you remember: OILRIG oxidation is loss, reduction is gain.
e.g. word equation:
chlorine + iodide ions → chloride ions + iodine
chemical equation:
$Cl_2 + 2I^- \rightarrow 2Cl^- + I_2$

22

Symbol equations

Symbol equations are shorter than word equations, but tell us much more. The symbol equation for burning methane is:

$CH_4 + 2O_2 \rightarrow CO_2 + 2H_2O$

These few characters tell us:
- the name and chemical formula (the **type** and **number** of atoms) of each substance
- the relative amounts, shown by numbers **in front** of each formula. (*Note: if there's only one, no number is shown.*)

The reactants (**one** methane molecule and **two** oxygen molecules) react with each other and are changed into the products (**one** carbon dioxide molecule and **two** water molecules). Atoms in the reactants are rearranged to make the products.

Question 2
What are the chemical formulae for (a) methane (b) oxygen (c) carbon dioxide (d) water?

Answer

How to write a chemical equation

Follow these steps. (See the worked example, right.)

- Write the word equation.

What's the chemical equation for the reaction between iron oxide and carbon monoxide?

Iron oxide + carbon monoxide → iron + carbon dioxide

- Replace names with formulae or symbols.

$Fe_2O_3 + CO \rightarrow Fe + CO_2$

- Check the number of atoms of each element on each side.

Reactants: $Fe_2O_3 + CO$
= 2 x Fe, 4 x O, 1 x C
Products: $Fe + CO_2$
= 1 x Fe, 1 x C, 2 x O

- If not equal, balance by doubling or trebling appropriate formulae.
  *Note: do **not alter** any of the formulae. Balance by putting numbers **in front**.*

CO needs 1 extra O to become CO_2
Fe_2O_3 has 3 x O, so can oxidise 3 x CO into 3 x CO_2
So, $Fe_2O_3 + 3CO \rightarrow Fe + 3CO_2$
To balance Fe_2O_3, we need 2Fe
So, the fully balanced equation is:
$Fe_2O_3 + 3CO \rightarrow 2Fe + 3CO_2$

Question 3
Write and balance the chemical equation for the reaction between nitrogen gas and hydrogen gas to make ammonia.

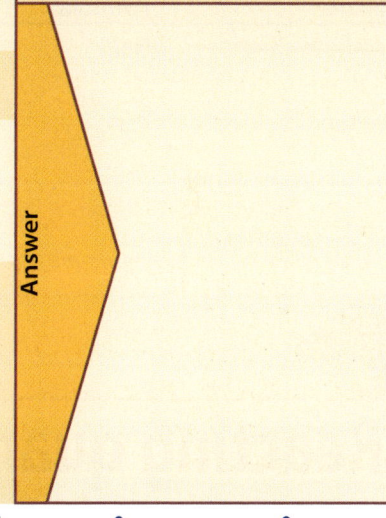

Answer

q&a

Q. Why do equations have to balance?

A. Chemical reactions can't create or destroy atoms. They only rearrange them into different substances. So, the equation must show the same number of atoms before reaction (in the reactants) and after reaction (in the products).

Q. *I get 'exothermic' and 'endothermic' confused. How can I remember which is which?*

A. Think of 'exit' for exo- (heat coming out) and 'into' for endo- (heat going in).

Exothermic and endothermic reactions

Burning a fuel gives out heat. So does mixing acid and alkali - the solution becomes warmer.

Combustion and neutralisation are **exothermic** reactions.

To decompose limestone it needs heat to be put in, so it's done in a kiln or furnace.

Photosynthesis needs energy from sunlight. These are **endothermic** reactions.

Useful equations ...

Burning methane	$CH_4 + 2O_2 \rightarrow CO_2 + 2H_2O$
Making iron: burning coke	$C + O_2 \rightarrow CO_2$
decomposing limestone	$CaCO_3 \rightarrow CaO + CO_2$
making carbon monoxide	$CO_2 + C \rightarrow 2CO$
reducing iron oxide	$Fe_2O_3 + 3CO \rightarrow 2Fe + 3CO_2$
Making lead	$PbO + CO \rightarrow Pb + CO_2$
Photosynthesis	$6CO_2 + 6H_2O \rightarrow C_6H_{12}O_6 + 6O_2$
Aerobic respiration	$C_6H_{12}O_6 + 6O_2 \rightarrow 6CO_2 + 6H_2O$
Anaerobic respiration (in muscles)	$C_6H_{12}O_6 \rightarrow 2C_3H_6O_3$
Anaerobic respiration (fermentation)	$C_6H_{12}O_6 \rightarrow 2C_2H_5OH + 2CO_2$

Chemistry applications

Reacting masses

Chemists need to be able to work out what quantities of chemicals react with one another and how much products are made. These quantities might be masses or volumes.

Relative masses

The **relative atomic mass** of an element is the number of times heavier its atoms are compared with hydrogen, the lightest element.

We use the same idea with compounds. We call it the **relative formula mass**. It's the number of times heavier all the atoms in a compound are compared with a hydrogen atom.

You can work it out by adding the relative atomic masses of the atoms shown in the chemical formula.

Name	Formula	Relative formula mass
sodium chloride	NaCl	1 Na atom and 1 Cl atom 23 + 35.5 = 58.5
ethane	C_2H_6	2 C atoms and 6 H atoms (2 x 12) + (6 x 1) = 30

Question 1
What is the relative formula mass of trichloromethane, $CHCl_3$?

Answer

Reacting quantities

Chemical equations tell us about the quantities of reactants and products in a reaction.

magnesium + chlorine → magnesium chloride

- relative atomic masses: Mg = 24 and Cl = 35.5
- relative formula masses: Cl_2 = 2 x 35.5 = 71 and $MgCl_2$ = 24 + (2 x 35.5) = 95
- chemical equation: Mg + Cl_2 → $MgCl_2$
- reacting masses: 24 g   71 g   95 g

So the chemical equation tells you that 24 g of magnesium reacts with 71 g of oxygen to make 95 g of magnesium chloride.

Counting atoms

Scientists count with a unit called the **mole**. To them, talking about a mole of magnesium oxide is the same as us talking about a pair of shoes or a dozen eggs. Ten moles of magnesium oxide is like saying ten dozen eggs.

However, a pair is just two and a dozen is just twelve. But a mole is a huge number:

602 000 000 000 000 000 000 000

which is also written as 6.02×10^{23}.

The mass of a mole of a substance is given by its relative formula mass in grams.

Question 3
(a) What is the mass of 1 mole of methane, CH_4?
(b) How many carbon atoms are there in 0.001 moles of carbon?

Answer

You can't count atoms. But - if you know the mass and formula of a substance - you can work out how many there are.

Using simple proportions you can work out other reacting quantities. For example:

12 g of magnesium reacts with 35.5 g of chlorine to make 47.5 g of magnesium chloride
2.4 g of magnesium reacts with 7.1 g of chlorine to make 9.5 g of magnesium chloride
240 g of magnesium reacts with 710 g of chlorine to make 950 g of magnesium chloride

Question 2
(a) What mass of magnesium is needed to make 190 g $MgCl_2$? (b) What mass of calcium oxide can be obtained from 10 g $CaCO_3$? [Relative atomic masses: Ca = 40; C = 12; O = 16] (c) What mass of carbon dioxide is produced when 50 g $CaCO_3$ reacts with an excess of dilute hydrochloric acid?

Answer

24

Quantities and amounts

In science-speak:
- **quantity** is something you measure, like length, time and mass
- **amount** is the number of moles of a substance.

One mole of calcium carbonate weighs 100 grams.

So if you weigh out 100 g (the **quantity**) of calcium carbonate you have one mole of calcium carbonate. And this is the **amount**.

Look at the formula $CaCO_3$. It tells you that one mole of calcium carbonate contains:
- one mole of calcium atoms
- one mole of carbon atoms
- three moles of oxygen atoms.

Question 4
(a) How many moles of calcium carbonate are there in 10 grams?
(b) How many moles of calcium atoms are there in 50 grams of calcium carbonate?
(c) How many moles of oxygen atoms are there in 5 grams of calcium carbonate?

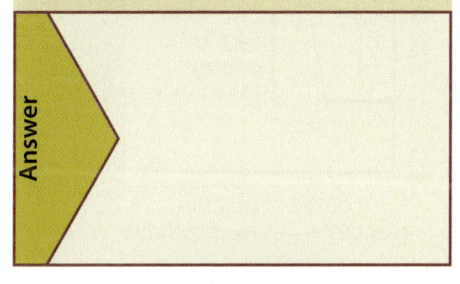

Answer

Quantities and units

Complete this list by adding the correct base SI unit to each quantity.

Quantity	SI Unit
Length	_____
Time	_____
Mass	_____
Temperature	_____
Electric current	_____

Reacting quantities using moles

To calculate quantities of reactants and products in a chemical reaction follow these steps:

1 Chemical equation
Write the chemical equation for the reaction (you don't need the state symbols, but you can include them if you want).

2 Quantities to amounts
Change the quantities of reactants or products into amounts of substance.

3 Using the equation
Use the equation to work out the amounts of other substance involved.

4 Amounts to quantities
Change these amounts back to quantities.

An example:
Calculate the mass of magnesium oxide that could be obtained when 12 g of magnesium is heated in oxygen.
- Relative atomic masses: magnesium = 24; oxygen = 16
- Relative formula mass of magnesium oxide = 24 + 16 = 40

1 Chemical equation
$2Mg + O_2 \rightarrow 2MgO$

2 Quantities to amounts
Amount of magnesium = $\frac{12}{24}$ = 0.5 moles

3 Using the equation

$2Mg + O_2 \rightarrow 2MgO$

2 moles of magnesium give 2 moles of magnesium oxide

So, 0.5 moles of magnesium gives 0.5 moles of magnesium oxide

4 Amounts to quantities
1 mole of magnesium oxide has mass (24 + 16) = 40 g
So 0.5 moles magnesium oxide has mass = 0.5 × 40 = 20 g

Question 5
Calculate the mass of:
(a) carbon dioxide; and
(b) water
produced when 8 g of methane is burnt.
Show your working.

Answer

Chemistry applications

Chemical change

When chemical changes occur heat is given out or taken in. How quickly and how far the reactions go depends on the reaction conditions.

How reactions happen

When substances react their particles must collide with one another. The more frequently they collide, the faster the reaction.

Imagine a mixture of hydrogen and chlorine. The molecules move around randomly, bumping into one another. The molecules move around at different speeds. The faster they move, the more energy they have.

Breaking and making bonds

When chemical reactions take place:
- Bonds between atoms in the reactants are broken.
  This **requires energy**.
- New bonds form between the atoms to make the products.
  This **gives out energy**.

Think about hydrogen and chlorine molecules bumping into one another. They **react** to make hydrogen chloride.

hydrogen + chlorine → hydrogen chloride

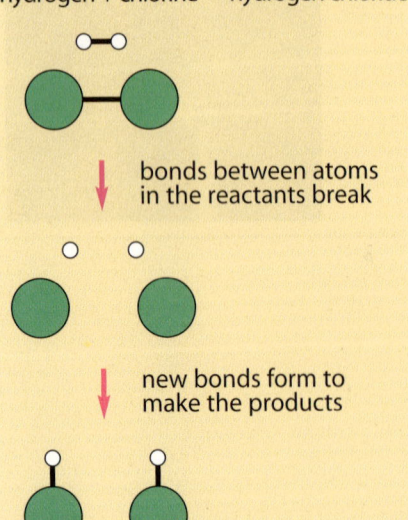

bonds between atoms in the reactants break

new bonds form to make the products

They need enough energy so bonds can be broken when they collide.

Exothermic and endothermic

Reactions that give out heat are **exothermic reactions**. The temperature of the reaction mixture increases. Think of **exo** as **exit**.

More energy is given out by new bonds forming than was needed to break the bonds in the reactants.

energy needed to break bonds / result: energy given out / energy released when bonds form
course of reaction: reactants → products

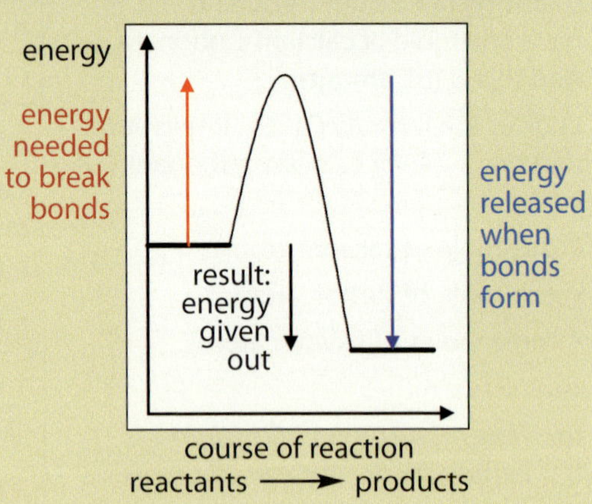

Reactions that take in heat are **endothermic reactions**. The temperature of the reaction mixture drops. Think of **endo** as **into**.

More energy is needed to break the bonds in the reactants.

energy needed to break bonds / result: energy taken in / energy released when bonds form
course of reaction: reactants → products

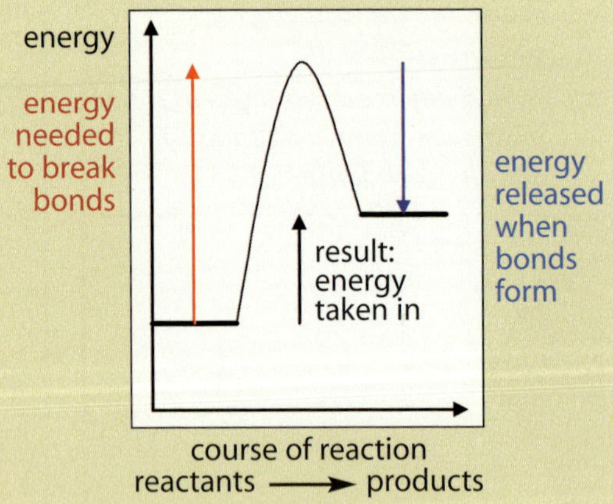

Question 1
Explain why:
(a) dilute hydrochloric acid gets hotter when sodium hydroxide solution is added to it
(b) a solution of citric acid gets colder when powdered sodium hydrogencarbonate is added to it.

Answer

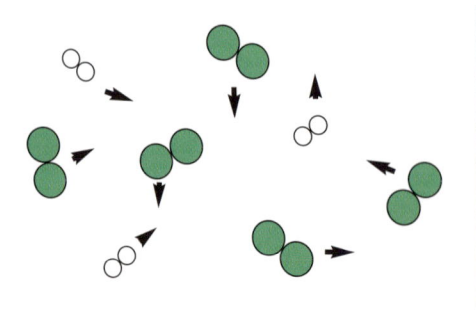

Catalysts

A catalyst is a substance that speeds up a chemical reaction, but remains unchanged at the end of the reaction.

Catalysts are vital to the chemical industry. They mean that lower temperatures and pressures can be used in manufacturing processes, and this reduces the cost.

Circle the two molecules likely to react first.

26

Reaction rate

The speed of the reaction (we also use the terms reaction rate and rate of reaction) depends on:

	low → high
concentration	——— reaction gets faster ——→
pressure	——— reaction gets faster ——→
temperature	——— reaction gets faster ——→

If the reaction is between a gas and a solid or a liquid and a solid, something else comes into play. It's the size of the particles of the solid.

Quite simply, the greater the surface area of the solid, the faster the reaction:

	large → small
particle size	——— reaction gets faster ——→

For example:
- copper sulfate powder dissolves in water more quickly than copper sulfate crystals
- dilute sulfuric acid reacts more quickly with zinc powder than with zinc granules
- calcium carbonate powder reacts faster than limestone chips with dilute hydrochloric acid.

Question 2
In each case, say which reaction is the fastest:
(a) *magnesium powder with dilute sulfuric acid at 20 °C or 40 °C*
(b) *a mixture of hydrogen and oxygen at a pressure of 10^5 Pa or 10^3 Pa*
(c) *limestone chips with 2 mol dm^{-3} hydrochloric acid or 0.2 mol dm^{-3} hydrochloric acid*
(d) *chlorine gas with aluminium powder or aluminium foil.*

Answer

Changing the balance

The position of equilibrium, in other words the relative amounts of reactants and products in the mixture, can be changed.

	proportion of ammonia in equilibrium mixture
	low — high
pressure	——— increasing pressure ——→
temperature	——— decreasing temperature ——→

Explanation:
- The number of molecules on the right hand side of the equation is less than the number on the left.

$$N_2 + 3H_2 \rightleftharpoons 2NH_3$$
    4 molecules   2 molecules

Increasing pressure always moves the balance to the side where there are fewer molecules.

- The reaction $N_2 + 3H_2 \rightarrow 2NH_3$ is exothermic. Increasing temperature always moves the balance towards the endothermic reaction.

Reversible reactions

Not all reactions go to completion. In other words, some of the reactants remain no matter how long the reaction mixture is left.

Let's look at the manufacture of ammonia:

$$N_2 + 3H_2 \rightarrow 2NH_3$$

No matter how long the mixture is left it always contains nitrogen, hydrogen and ammonia.

You can picture it like this:
- nitrogen molecules collide with hydrogen molecules to make ammonia:

$$N_2 + 3H_2 \rightarrow 2NH_3$$

- ammonia molecules collide with one another to make nitrogen and hydrogen:

$$2NH_3 \rightarrow N_2 + 3H_2$$

The reactions keep see-sawing until the rate of both is the same. At this point we say the three substances are in dynamic equilibrium.

We show this by writing:

$$N_2 + 3H_2 \rightleftharpoons 2NH_3$$

$\rightleftharpoons$ is used to show the reaction is in dynamic equilibrium.

You might try to imagine it like a runner on a treadmill. Both the runner and the treadmill are moving, but in opposite directions. When they move at the same speed it looks as if the person is running on the spot.

Conditions for making ammonia

Ammonia is made under high pressure at 350 - 550 °C with a catalyst (iron oxide).

The high pressure increases the proportion of ammonia in the equilibrium mixture. The temperature is chosen is a compromise:

- a low temperature increases the proportion of ammonia
- a high temperature increases the speed of the reaction.

Chemistry applications

▶ ▶ ▶ ▶

Getting metals from ores

Metals are obtained from their ores by reduction.

Chemical and physical methods

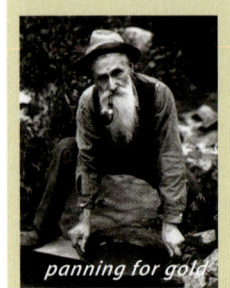

Gold occurs in the earth 'native' - as gold metal itself, not as compounds. We just need to crush the rock to release the tiny pieces of gold. This is physical extraction.

Most other metals are found as compounds. They need chemical reactions to extract them from their ores.

We use the same type of chemical process to obtain iron, lead and several other metals from their ores. We heat the metal oxide with carbon.

panning for gold

metal oxide + carbon → metal + carbon dioxide

Carbon takes oxygen away from the metal oxide. This is **reduction**. It **reduces** the amount of oxygen. Coke is used to provide the carbon. The carbon gains oxygen. This is **oxidation**.

Question 1
(a) What is an ore? (b) Name one common ore of iron and one of lead.

Answer

Extracting iron

Making iron is an important industrial process because we use more iron than any other metal. Most iron is turned into steel. Steel is an alloy which is much stronger than pure iron.

Question 2
What is an alloy?

Answer

Iron ore is a mixture of iron oxide, Fe_2O_3, and various impurities. Iron is extracted in a blast furnace.

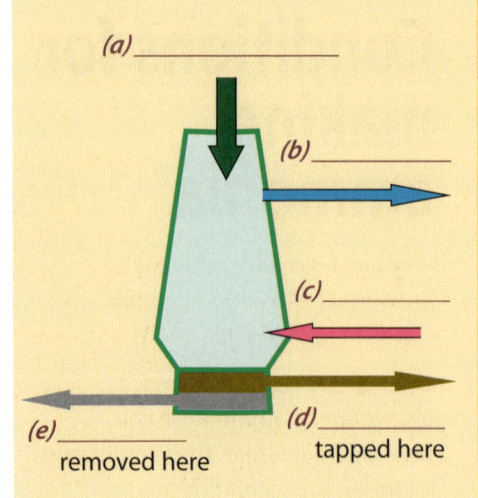

(a) _____
(b) _____
(c) _____
(e) _____ removed here
(d) _____ tapped here

Label the diagram, choosing from this list of words: hot waste gases; slag; raw materials; hot air blast; iron

- The furnace runs continuously.
- Three raw materials (iron ore, coke and limestone) are tipped into the top of the furnace. Coke provides the carbon.
- A blast of hot air is blown in near the bottom.
- Coke burns, heating the furnace to over 1500 °C:

  C + O_2 → CO_2
  carbon   oxygen   carbon dioxide

- More coke reduces carbon dioxide to carbon monoxide:

  C + CO_2 → $2CO$
  carbon   carbon dioxide   carbon monoxide

- Carbon monoxide reduces iron oxide to iron. This reaction also oxidises carbon monoxide to carbon dioxide:

  Fe_2O_3 + $3CO$ → $2Fe$ + $3CO_2$
  iron oxide   carbon monoxide   iron   carbon dioxide

- Molten iron trickles down into the bottom of the furnace, and is tapped (run off) regularly.
- Limestone, $CaCO_3$, decomposes into two products:

  $CaCO_3$ → CaO + CO_2
  limestone   calcium oxide   carbon dioxide

- CO_2 reacts with carbon to provide more CO for reducing iron oxide.
- CaO combines with impurities in the ore to make slag.

Question 3
(a) What is the chemical name for limestone? (b) How is the in-coming air blast heated? (c) Name the two main waste gases that come out of a blast furnace.

Answer

Aluminium from bauxite

Bauxite is an ore of aluminium. It's essentially aluminium oxide, Al_2O_3. Aluminium oxide cannot be reduced by heating it with carbon.

Instead, aluminium oxide is melted and electricity passed through the liquid.

Molten aluminium oxide consists of aluminium ions, Al^{3+}, and oxide ions, O^{2-}, moving around relatively freely. When an electric current passes:

At the cathode (negative electrode):

$Al^{3+} + 3e^- \rightarrow Al$

aluminium ions gain electrons: reduction

At the anode (positive electrode):

$2O^{2-} \rightarrow O_2 + 4e^-$

Oxide ions lose electrons: oxidation

The overall reaction is:

$2Al_2O_3 \rightarrow 4Al + 3O_2$

Question 5
Sodium is obtained by the electrolysis of molten sodium chloride.
(a) Write equations for what happens
   (i) at the cathode
   (ii) at the anode.
(b) What is the overall reaction?

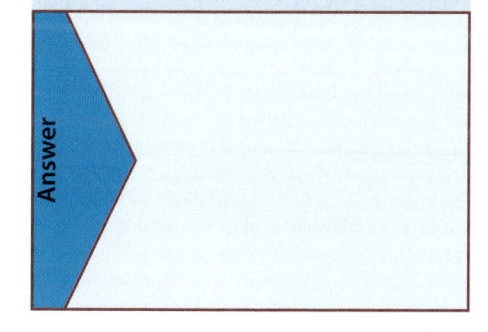

Extracting lead

- Lead ore is lead sulfide, PbS, rather than lead oxide, PbO.
- Roasting the ore in air converts it to lead oxide.
- Lead is extracted in the same way as iron, but in smaller blast furnaces.
- As in iron extraction, it's carbon monoxide that reduces the lead oxide.

Write the names of the chemicals in the spaces provided ...

PbO   +   CO   →   Pb   + CO_2

Question 4
Suggest what happens to the sulfur in lead sulfide when the ore is roasted to form lead oxide.

q & a

Q. I get confused by oxidation and reduction. My teacher says you can't have one without the other, but books often describe a reaction as just being reduction or oxidation. Who's right?

A. **Reduction** and **oxidation** always take place together. It's often called a **redox** reaction. Any oxygen lost by one compound must be gained by something else. We often focus on only one half of the redox reaction - whichever gives the product we want. However, the other half must happen too.

Examples from iron extraction:

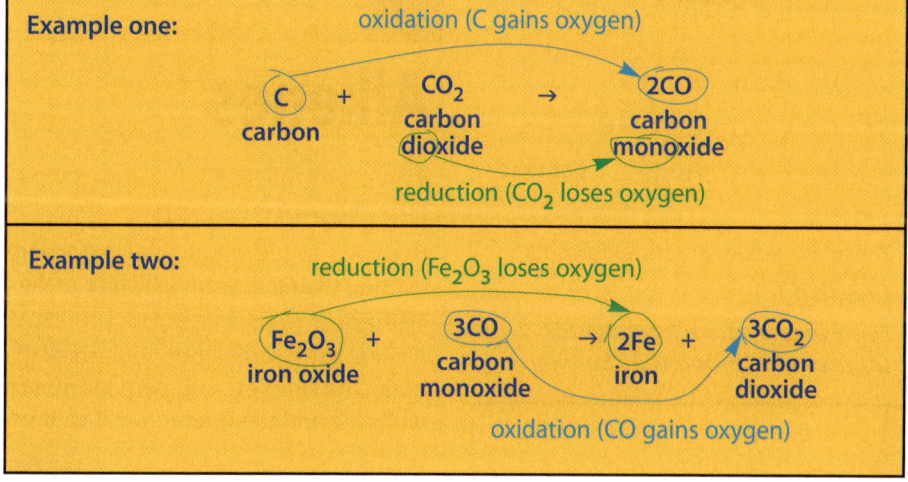

Example one:

oxidation (C gains oxygen)

C + CO_2 → 2CO
carbon   carbon dioxide   carbon monoxide

reduction (CO_2 loses oxygen)

Example two:

reduction (Fe_2O_3 loses oxygen)

Fe_2O_3 + 3CO → 2Fe + $3CO_2$
iron oxide   carbon monoxide   iron   carbon dioxide

oxidation (CO gains oxygen)

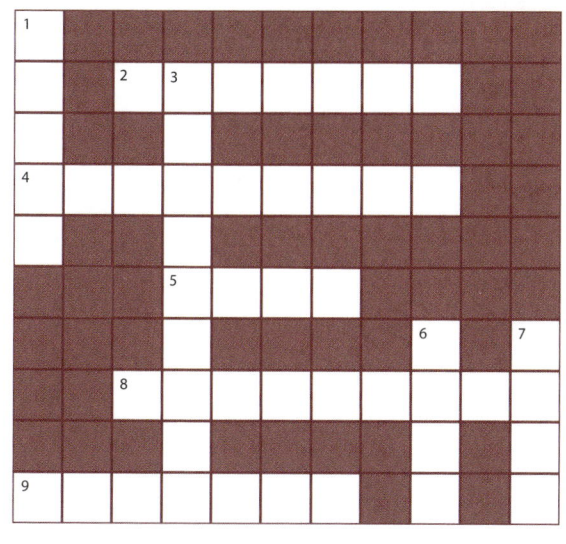

Complete this crossword:

Across:

2, 5 and 8 across.
  These are the three raw materials tipped into the top of the furnace when extracting iron.

4. When carbon gains oxygen and forms carbon dioxide, this is called _____.

5. See 2 across.

8. See 2 across.

9. Iron is extracted in a blast _____.

Down:

1. When reduction and oxidation both take place, it is sometimes called a _____ reaction.

3. When carbon takes oxygen away from a metal oxide it is called _____, because it reduces the amount of oxygen.

6. This precious metal is found in the ground as an element.

7. The formula for this element's ore is PbS.

Chemistry applications

Organic compounds

Alkanes

Alkanes are hydrocarbons with the general formula C_nH_{2n+2}.
Each carbon atom is bonded to four other atoms. These are carbon or hydrogen atoms.

Name	molecular formula
methane	CH_4
ethane	C_2H_6
propane	C_3H_8
butane	C_4H_{10}
pentane	C_5H_{12}
hexane	C_6H_{14}
heptane	C_7H_{16}
octane	C_8H_{18}

We represent the arrangement of atoms using 2D drawings like these:

```
    H
    |
H − C − H      methane
    |
    H
```

```
  H   H   H   H   H
  |   |   |   |   |
H−C − C − C − C − C−H       pentane
  |   |   |   |   |
  H   H   H   H   H
```

These are called structural formula.

Question 1
Draw the structural formulae for (a) ethane (b) propane (c) butane.

Answer

Three-dimensional shapes

The *flat* pictures of structural formulae don't tell us everything. Molecules are three-dimensional:

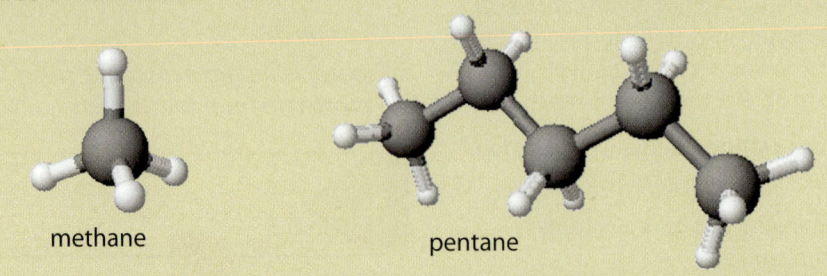

methane   pentane

Even these don't tell the whole story. The single covalent bonds between atoms are free to rotate. This means the carbon chains can twist, changing the shape of the molecule. However, each carbon atom is always surrounded by four other atoms at the corners of a tetrahedron.

Question 2
What four atoms surround a carbon atom (a) at the end of a propane molecule; (b) in the middle of a propane molecule?

Answer

Alkenes

Alkanes are important fuels. For example, methane (natural gas) burns in air:

$CH_4 + 2O_2 \rightarrow CO_2 + 2H_2O$

However, on the whole they're not very reactive. This means they're not useful starting materials from which to make other organic compounds. Instead, alkenes are used.

Alkenes are hydrocarbon molecules that have a carbon-carbon double covalent bond. The simplest, and perhaps most important, is ethene, C_2H_4. It's a flat molecule and the double bond cannot rotate.

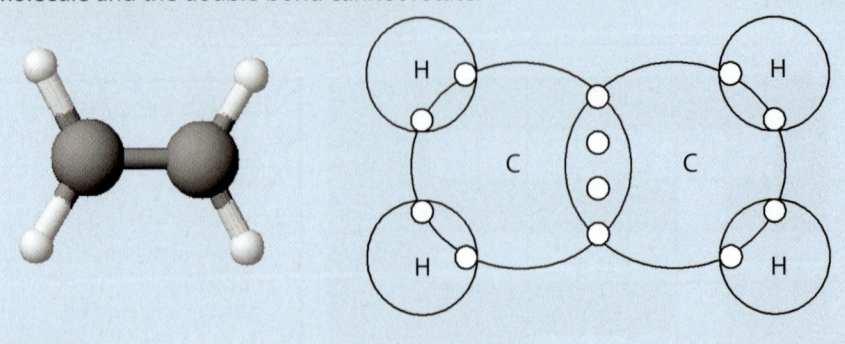

Question 3
What is the general formula for an alkene?

Answer

30

Cracking

Ethene and other alkenes are made by **cracking fractions** obtained from the **distillation** of crude oil. Cracking means breaking down large molecules into smaller molecules.

For example:

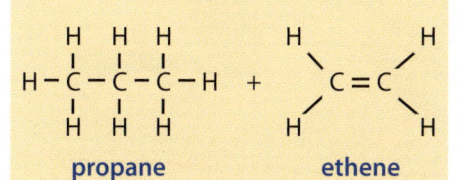

pentane

↓

propane + ethene

The alkane is heated strongly and passed over a catalyst. Count the carbon and hydrogen atoms to check that none have been lost.

Question 4
Name three substances obtained when butane is cracked.

1 _____

2 _____

3 _____

Have a look at these photos of ball and stick models.

Photo 1 shows a decane molecule.

Photo 2 shows the decane molecule broken into two smaller molecules, octane and ethene.

This process happens in a catalytic cracker.

Check that no hydrogen and carbon atoms are lost in the process.

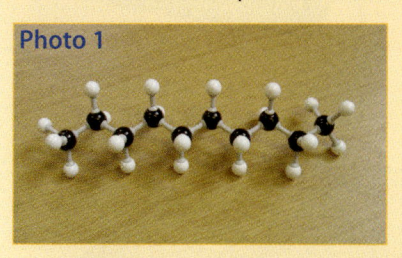

Photo 1

Photo 2

Reactions of ethene

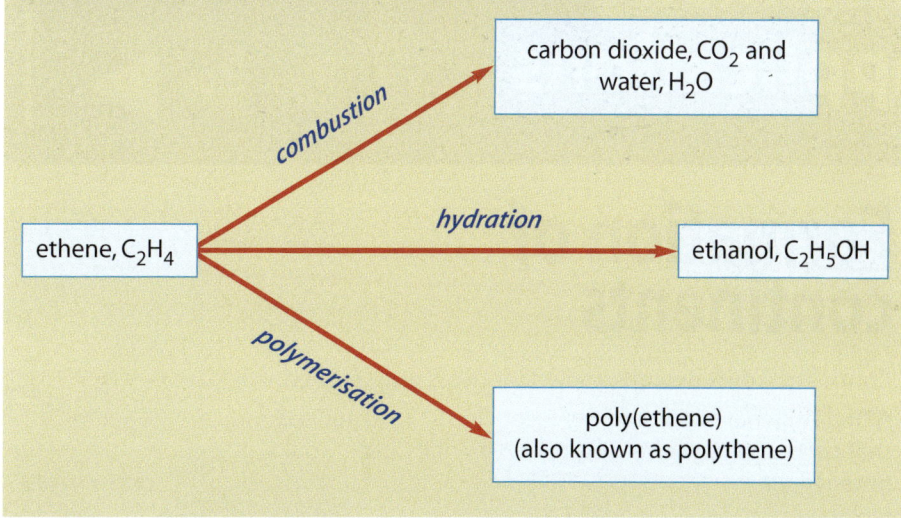

ethene, C_2H_4
- combustion → carbon dioxide, CO_2 and water, H_2O
- hydration → ethanol, C_2H_5OH
- polymerisation → poly(ethene) (also known as polythene)

Chloroethene

Chloroethene is like ethene, except one hydrogen atom is replaced by a chlorine atom. Its molecular formula is C_2H_3Cl. Like ethene, it polymerises. Poly(chloroethene) is formed, commonly known as PVC.

Uses of PVC: building materials (such as pipes, window frames, floor coverings and barrier sheets); in health services and medical appliances (such as transfusion and blood bags and blister packaging); electrical cable sheathing, automotive underbody protective coatings, balls, dolls, conveyor belts and tarpaulins.

Alcohols, carboxylic acids and esters

Alcohols are organic compounds with a hydroxyl group, -OH. The most common one is **ethanol**, C_2H_5OH. It's made by **fermentation** of sugar or by the hydration of ethene.

Uses of ethanol: alcoholic drinks, cosmetics, inks and coatings, and biofuel. With supplies of fossil fuels running out, ethanol made by fermenting sugar cane or sugar beet is a useful alternative to fossil fuels.

Carboxylic acids are organic compounds with a carboxylic acid group, -COOH. The most common one is **ethanoic acid**, CH_3COOH.

Uses of ethanoic acid: pickling and making esters.

Alcohols react with carboxylic acids to make esters. For example:

ethanol + ethanoic acid → ethyl ethanoate + water

Ethyl ethanoate is an ester. However, the reaction is not neutralisation and an ester is not a salt.

Uses of esters: solvents and fragrances.

	appearance	boiling point / °C	solubility in water	pH of solution
ethanol	colourless liquid, smells of alcohol	79	completely soluble	7
ethanoic acid	colourless liquid, smells of vinegar	118	completely soluble	about 4
ethyl ethanoate	colourless liquid, has a fruity smell	77	insoluble	7

31

Chemistry applications

Our changing planet

Formation of continents

Continental drift describes how continents were formed.

Alfred Wegener suggested the theory in 1912. He noticed that continents on either side of the Atlantic Ocean would fit together.

Fossil evidence also suggested that long ago one massive continent existed (called **Pangaea**). Fossils of the same creatures were found in different continents. They couldn't have travelled between the two places unless the land masses were once joined (see diagram).

Wegener's theory of continental drift wasn't accepted until the 1960s, when new evidence described how land masses move on **tectonic plates**.

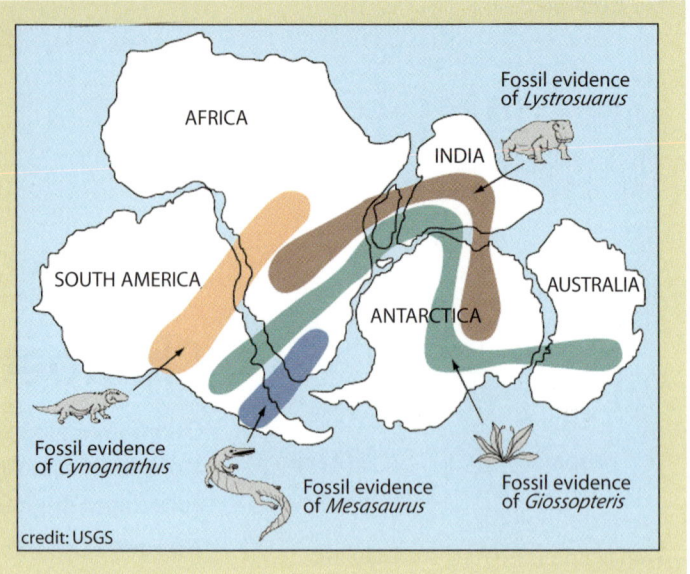

Tectonic plates

The outer layer of the Earth is the **lithosphere**. This is a jigsaw of **tectonic plates** that move over a layer of semi-molten magma. It's this movmenet that forms continents and mountains, and causes volcanoes, earthquakes and tsumnamis. The *solid* uppermost of the lithosphere is the **crust**.

This bridge in Iceland crosses the boundary of the Eurasian and North American continental tectonic plates.

Plate movements

There are three main types of tectonic plate movements. They have different effects on the Earth's crust ...

1. **Plates moving *past* each other**

    The plates don't pass each other easily and can get stuck together. Over time the pressure gradually increases. Eventually the plates suddenly release causing massive vibrations called an **earthquake**.

2. **Plates moving *away* from each other**

    This normally happens under the ocean. As the plates separate, the gap fills with molten lava from below. It hardens and forms new crust. This is **seafloor spreading**. Sometimes the spreading happens at different rates along the boundary causing fractures of the crust and underwater earthquakes.

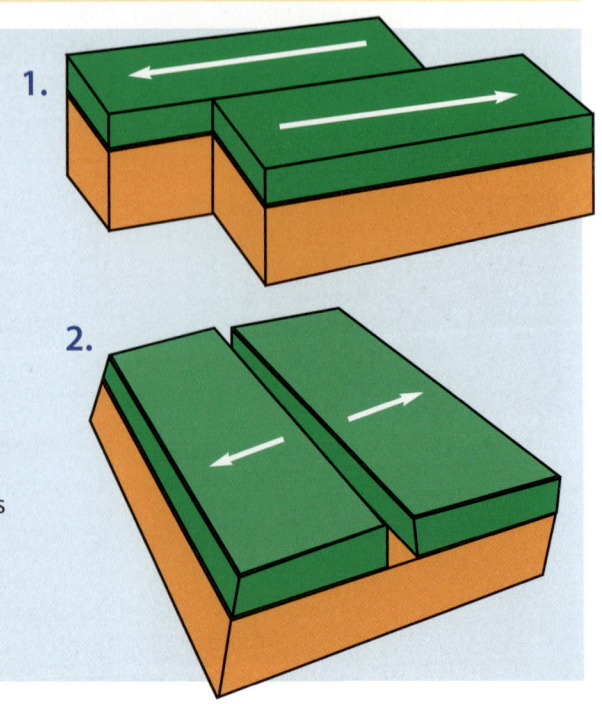

3. Plates moving *towards* each other

Oceanic plates are denser than continental plates.

So, when they collide, the oceanic plate **subducts** under the continental plate. During subduction, pressure can build up. If it suddenly releases, it causes an earthquake and the level of the sea-bed may rise.

Where plates collide, ground levels may rise and molten lava may erupt from a volcano.

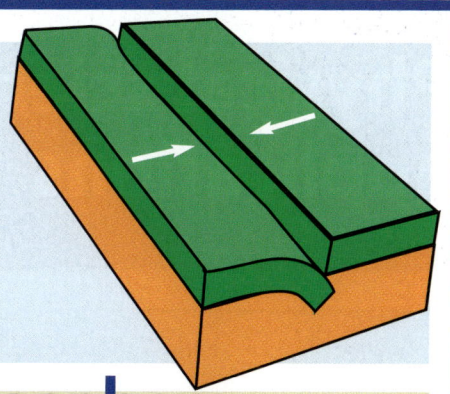

Driving forces of plate movement

Convection currents

When a fluid is heated, its molecules move faster and its volume increases.

The number of molecules stays the same even though the volume increases. And so the density decreases.

The less dense fluid rises above cooler, denser fluid. This is called **convection**.

Convection occurs in the earth. A difference in temperature between the hot core and cooler surface causes convection currents.

Plate movement occurs as the plates *ride* these convection currents.

Gravity

Convection currents may not provide enough energy to move the large plates. Gravity may also play a role.

Gravity causes cold, dense oceanic crust to sink when it slides under another plate. This pulls the rest of the plate with it.

Thermal plumes

Another theory is that narrow plumes of deep molten fluid rise at hotspots (normally near triple ridge junctions) causing stresses on the plates and movement.

The Himalaya mountains in Asia are still growing. Why is this?

Answer

The Earth's atmosphere

The Earth's atmosphere is made of:

21%	oxygen (O_2)
78%	nitrogen (N_2)
0.04%	carbon dioxide (CO_2)
~0.9%	argon (Ar)

plus trace amounts of other gases and water vapour.

The atmosphere is essential for life. Changes, such as destruction of the ozone layer or build up of greenhouse gases caused by human activities, could be extremely damaging to the planet.

The origin of the atmosphere

Atmospheric gases originated from the Earth's core during volcanic eruptions. Oxygen was released from the CO_2 by **photosynthesis** in green plants and algae.

Over time, more and more photosynthetic organisms grew, increasing the amount of oxygen. This changed the make-up of the atmosphere.

Today **photosynthesis**, **respiration** and **combustion** help maintain the amounts of each gas present in the atmosphere.

Volcanic gases

About 1-5% of volcanic emissions are gases. The most abundant are water vapour, carbon dioxide and sulfur dioxide.

Living close to a volcano can be dangerous. Volcanic gases, as well as hot lava, can be harmful to humans, animals, plants, crops and property ...

Acidic gas

Acidic gases mix with rain water producing acid rain. It burns vegetation and can contaminate drinking water.

Carbon dioxide

Carbon dioxide is a greenhouse gas. It causes global warming. If it collects in poorly ventilated places it can cause suffocation.

Sulfur dioxide

Sulfur dioxide can cause global cooling, destroy ozone and create volcanic smog (vog). Breathing in vog causes problems, such as eye damage and respiratory problems. Extreme exposure can lead to death.

Physical science applications ▶▶▶▶ | Conservation of energy

Energy comes in various forms. Some forms are useful, others are less useful. Being able to change energy from one form to another is important.

Energy and fuels

There are two types of energy stored in fuels:
- **chemical energy** (stored in fossil fuels, but also in food and batteries)
- **nuclear energy** (stored in the nuclei of atoms).

Question 1
What form of energy is stored in an apple?

Answer ▶

Other forms of energy

Energy comes in many forms. As well as chemical and nuclear, it may be:
- **kinetic energy** - the energy an object has because of its movement (movement energy)
- **potential energy** - when something is moved (lifted, stretched or squashed), kinetic energy is changed to potential energy (position energy)
- **heat energy** (thermal energy) 
- **light energy**
- **sound energy**.

And finally … there is **electricity** or **electrical** energy.

Question 2
What kind of energy is stored in (a) natural gas (b) a stretched rubber band (c) a battery (d) running water?

Answer ▶

Transferring energy

Energy can be changed from one form to another. This is often called **transferring energy**. You can show this with an **energy transfer diagram**. These show:
- energy input and energy output
- the process by which the transfer takes place.

Look right to see an energy transfer diagram for a torch bulb.

Importantly, when energy is transferred none is lost and no extra energy is produced. You end up with exactly the same amount as you started with - just in different forms.

This is the **law of conservation of energy**. Energy cannot be created or destroyed. Quite simply:

Input energy = output energy

Complete the energy transfer diagram for a stereo (right).

input energy → electrical energy 
Transfer takes place in the light bulb
→ output energy / light energy

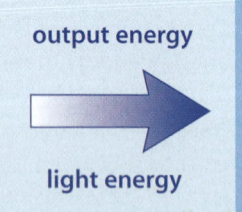

input energy → A _____ energy 
Transfer takes place in the stereo
→ output energy / B _____ energy

NOTE: The correct expression is **transforming energy**, rather than transferring energy. However, both expressions are used. Strictly, transfer means **moving energy from one place to another without changing its form**. For example, heat can be transferred by convection, conduction or radiation.

Molecular theory

Particles are constantly in motion.

In a **solid** they vibrate about fixed positions in a lattice.

In a **liquid** they move randomly, but close to one another.

In a **gas** they move randomly about ten times further from one another than they are in a liquid.

Any substance has **internal energy**. This is made up of:
- energy due to the bonds between particles (potential energy)
- energy due to movement of particles (kinetic energy).

How much they move depends on the temperature.

Change of state

A substance changes state, e.g. from a solid to a liquid, if it's given enough energy to overcome its internal energy.

Heat a solid and its particles vibrate more vigorously. Heat it enough and you overcome the bonding between particles. They become free to move. This is what happens when something melts. The solid becomes a liquid.

Heat a liquid and its particles move faster and faster. Heat it enough the particles escape from the liquid and form a gas. This is what happens when something boils. The liquid becomes a gas.

Find the six words which, when put in the correct order, state the law of conservation of energy.

D	Y	B	N	T	Z	D	G	K	F
Y	E	T	X	M	F	A	X	C	V
U	G	Y	I	C	Y	D	R	T	I
E	E	B	O	G	D	E	Q	O	J
V	S	W	R	R	A	P	N	N	G
R	T	E	J	T	T	O	B	N	M
K	N	G	E	F	R	S	W	A	D
E	J	D	I	A	A	C	E	C	M
S	L	K	Z	L	I	E	Z	D	I
M	A	A	J	Z	W	S	D	J	Z

Conserving energy

Switch on a light and you will start to transform electrical energy into light energy. But that's not the whole story. If you put your hand near a lit bulb you will feel the heat it's giving off. Be careful - do not touch the bulb!

What's happening is that the electrical energy is being transformed by the bulb to light and heat. From the law of conservation of energy:

input energy = output energy

So in the light bulb, the following change takes place:

electrical energy = light energy + heat energy

Since the purpose of the light bulb is to provide light, we say the heat energy is wasted. In general we might write:

output energy = useful energy + wasted energy

Another way of saying this is that the input energy has been **transformed** and spreads out into more than one form of energy. This is always the case.

Question 3
(a) What is the output energy of a light bulb made up of?
(b) A television uses electrical energy. Into what forms of energy does it transform this?

Answer

Spreading out of energy

You might come across a diagram like this to show how energy spreads out when it's transformed.

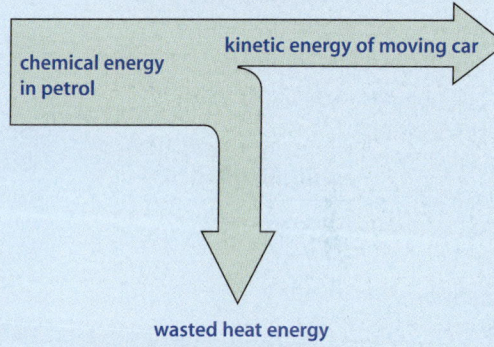

Question 4
(a) If the input energy (from the petrol) in a car is 500,000 joules, what is the output energy?
(b) If the kinetic energy produced is 200,000 joules, how much energy is wasted as heat?

A Sankey diagram:

chemical energy in petrol → kinetic energy of moving car
↓ wasted heat energy

Answer

q & a

Q. *We can't create energy, nor destroy it. So how can we be running short of energy? And why do we need to develop new energy resources?*

A. When we use energy we don't use it up. It's changed from one form to another. In any energy transform, one of the forms is always heat energy. Sometimes this is what's needed. However, often it's not and it's wasted energy that spreads out into the atmosphere.

Energy isn't destroyed. It's just not in a useful form any more. Remember: input energy = output energy = useful energy + wasted energy (often heat energy).

It's not energy that's running short, it's energy resources such as fossil fuels.

Before supplies run out we need to find new ones or look for alternatives. We also need to use existing supplies as efficiently as possible.

35

Physical science applications

Energy loss and heat transfer

Changing energy from one form in to another in a device or machine needs to be efficient as possible. In other words, we want as much as possible in the useful form and as little as possible wasted.

Being efficient

Being efficient means getting the most out of the time and energy you spend doing something. It's about not wasting time and energy. It's the same with mechanical and electrical appliances. They are designed to transform one form of energy into another form. As you've learned, during transformation, the energy gets spread out. More than one form is produced.

Measuring efficiency

We want mechanical and electrical appliances to be as efficient as possible. But how can we measure efficiency?

We can

- measure the energy put into a device - it's the input energy
- measure the amount of energy that comes in the form we want it. It's called the useful energy
- calculate the efficiency using the formula:

$$\text{efficiency} = \frac{\text{useful energy} \times 100}{\text{input energy}} \%$$

Question 1
What is 'output energy'?

Answer

Question 2
What is the efficiency of a machine where the input energy equals the useful energy produced?

Answer

Working out efficiency

The engine of a car changes the chemical energy of petrol into kinetic energy. One gram (1 g) of petrol contains about 40 000 joules of energy. Suppose that when the car uses 1 g of petrol its engine produces 16 000 joules of kinetic energy. What is its efficiency?

Input energy = 40 000 joules

Useful energy = 16 000 joules

Therefore,

$$\text{efficiency} = \frac{16\,000 \times 100}{40\,000} = 40\,\%$$

Hint: if you do this type of calculation and get an answer greater than 100% something went wrong! The most likely explanation is that you put the input and useful energy the wrong way round.

Question 3
A coal-burning power station converts every 2000 joules of chemical energy in the coal to 780 joules of electrical energy.
(a) How much energy is wasted from 2000 joules of chemical energy?
(a) What form of energy is this wasted energy?
(c) What is the efficiency of the power station?

Answer

Did you know? For hundreds of years people have tried to make perpetual motion machines (machines that, once started, keep moving without more input energy). Great idea, but can it done?

Friction

The major cause of low efficiency in a machine is **friction** between the moving parts.

They rub together and generate heat. This is why the moving parts are usually lubricated with oil or graphite powder.

But no matter how well lubricated they are, there is always some friction and, therefore, energy wasted as heat.

This is about the efficiency of heat transfer. Find the five words needed to complete the formulae (below, right).

```
          Y I L
        X C B N Y
      G Q N B J P Q
    S P I E M J Q U E
    A F G I O E X T T
    G T G C G W S A N
    J U S I P A W U C
    Z P J F W Y E W N
    C T J F L Z Y E M
      U Z E U S L H
      O U J F G H P
        L G E X Y
        T Y S U G
          T U V
          W O S
          V B E
```

A bright idea

Ordinary light bulbs (tungsten filament) are notoriously inefficient. Only about 10% of the electrical energy is changed into light energy. The rest becomes heat energy.

Fluorescent strip lights have been around for ages. They are cheaper to run than filament light bulbs, but they are big and can be unsightly. But now we have high efficiency bulbs (also called low energy light bulbs). These combine the advantages of filament bulbs and fluorescent strip lighting, but without the disadvantages.

In short, high efficiency bulbs use less energy and last longer.

So what's the catch? Well, they cost more to buy. However, a few sums will show the higher cost of buying is more than paid back by the savings on the electricity bill. And lighting makes up 10-15% of the electricity bill in most homes.

Calculations

If electricity costs 6 p per kWh, then:

- to buy and run ten 100 watt filament bulbs each for 1000 hours (a total of 10 000 hours) costs about £63:
  - *100 W for 10 000 hours = 1000 kWh*
  - *one bulb = 30 p*
  - *so, (10 x 30 p) + (1000 x 6 p) = £63.*

- to buy and run one 20 watt high efficiency bulb for 10 000 hours costs about £18:
  - *20 W for 10 000 hours = 200 kWh*
  - *one bulb = £6*
  - *so, £6 + (200 x 6 p) = £18.*

The savings (£45) are plain to see.

---

ordinary lightbulbs   high efficiency lightbulbs

Bulb facts

20 watt high efficiency bulbs ...

- give the same amount of light as 100 watt filament bulbs
- last 10 000 hours (100 watt filament bulbs last 1000 hours)
- cost about £6 (100 watt filament bulbs cost about 30 p).

Wordsearch formulae ...

_ _ _ _ _ _ _ _ _ _ = $\dfrac{\_ \_ \_ \_ \_ \_ \text{ energy} \times 100}{\_ \_ \_ \_ \_ \text{ energy}}$ %

_ _ _ _ _ _ energy = useful energy - _ _ _ _ _ _ energy

---

q & a

Q. Why should I buy high efficiency appliances?

A. They use less energy.

This means you save money and ...

... power stations need to produce less energy

... power stations use less fuel and produce less pollution

... the Earth's supplies will last longer while we try to find alternative supplies and our environment will be cleaner.

You know it makes sense!

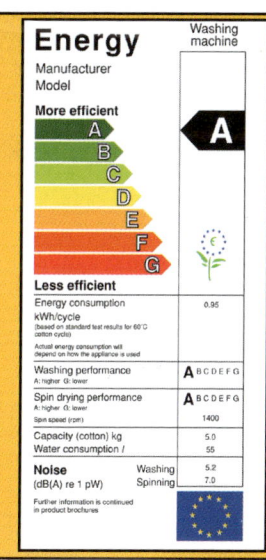

Q. OK, I'm persuaded. I want to use energy efficiently. But how do I know what electrical appliances to buy?

A. The European Union (EU) Energy Label (see picture, left) rates the efficiency of appliances, so look out for it. By law it must be shown on all domestic fridges, freezers and fridge-freezers, washing machines, electric tumble dryers, combined washer-dryers, dishwashers and lightbulbs.

The rating goes from a rating of **A** (most efficient) to **G** (least efficient).

37

Physical science applications

Conduction, convection and radiation

Often we want to keep things cool or hot. In other words, we want to slow down the movement of heat. To do this effectively, scientists need to understand how heat can be transferred from one place to another.

Heat transfer: from hot to cold

Heat energy moves from a hot place (high temperature) to a cold place (low temperature). It can't happen the other way. Heat can transfer in three ways: **conduction**, **convection** and **radiation**.

Conduction

The main way heat energy is transferred in a solid is conduction.

- Atoms in a solid vibrate about their fixed positions in a lattice. They constantly hit their neighbouring atoms.
- The more heat energy they are given, the more they vibrate.
- If one end of a solid is heated its atoms vibrate more. They hit their neighbours and transfer some of the energy.
- The heat energy is transferred from atom to atom along the solid. The other end of the solid gets hot.

Some solids are good conductors of heat. Others are not.

Metal frying pans conduct heat well: heat energy is transferred from the cooker to the food easily.

The handles are made of poor conductors of heat, such as wood or plastic.

Question 1
What is a poor conductor of heat called?

Answer

Radiation

It's what you feel when you put your hand close to (but not touching) something that's hot.

Radiation has an important property. It doesn't need a solid, liquid or gas to pass through. It can pass through empty space - just like light. And like light it can be reflected from a shiny surface.

Shiny objects radiate less heat energy than dark, dull ones.

The radiant energy is infrared. Most ovens, grills and toasters cook food using infrared radiation.

Question 2
Why is it a good idea to put shiny foil behind a radiator?

Answer

Question 3
How is most of the heat transferred in metal objects?

Answer

Convection

Gases and liquids conduct heat energy because their particles move and collide with one another. However, heat energy also spreads out in gases and liquids by convection.

- The molecules in air move around.
- As they are given heat energy they move faster.
- When the molecules are moving slowly they stay closer together than when they are moving faster. So cold air is denser ('heavier') than hot air.
- When air is heated, it becomes less dense. It rises, to be replaced by colder air.
- This colder air gets warm and rises, and so the process goes on.

It's the same in other gases and in liquids.

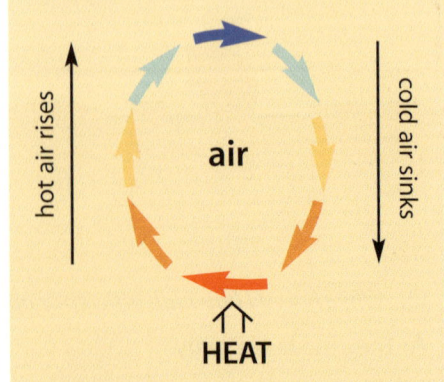

A mirage is caused by convection. The air above a hot tarmac road in the summer shimmers. It looks almost like water. What you are seeing is convection. The air gets hot and rises, being replaced by colder air which in turn gets hot and rises.

A mirage is caused by convection.

Forced convection

You may have seen, or even have one at home, convection heaters. Anything used to heat a room or other space works by convection - hot air rising and cool air sinking.

But what we buy as convection heaters have a small fan that speeds up the circulation of the warm air. So, it's not just natural convection. It's **forced convection**.

Question 6
Look at aluminium foil and you'll see it has a shiny side and a dull side.

If you wanted to wrap a piece of hot chicken in aluminium foil to keep it warm for a picnic, would you use the foil with the shiny side or the dull side facing the warm chicken piece?

Answer

Cutting your losses

Energy should be used efficiently. One way is to minimise heat losses.

Insulation
Insulation is the answer to heat loss by **conduction**. We wrap the thing we want to keep hot in an insulating material. We **insulate** it:

- take away food
- buildings
- hot water pipes in houses and factories
- and ourselves!

We also insulate things to keep them cool: cool boxes to keep food and drink cold.

Wood, plastic and ceramics are good insulators. Metals are not.

Trapped air is a good insulator. Many of the materials we use for insulation have air trapped inside them. Examples are: woollen clothing, foam polystyrene and bubble wrap.

Keeping out draughts
Convection happens naturally in gases and liquids. It can also be forced (for example, a convector heater has a fan to increase the speed hot air is spread around a room).

If it's cold outside, warm air 'escapes' from a room if there is a gap for it to get through. A wind blowing outside an open window will increase the speed of convection of hot air from a room. This is where draught excluders are useful. They reduce heat loss by convection.

Shiny surfaces
Shiny surfaces are the answer to cutting heat losses by **radiation**. Radiation is reflected by silvery shiny surfaces. A vacuum flask has a silvery inside to reduce heat loss by radiation.

Question 4
Complete this diagram of a vacuum flask:

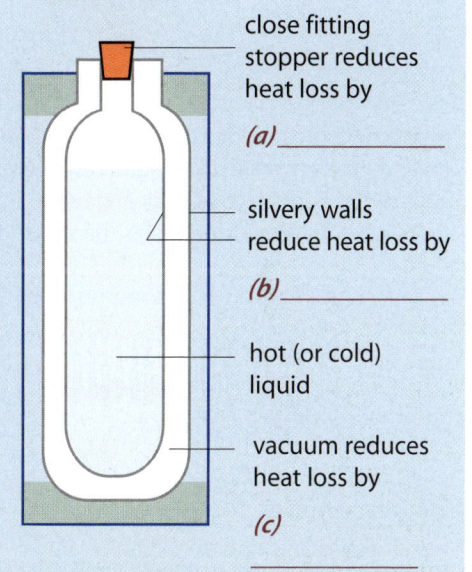

close fitting stopper reduces heat loss by

(a)_____

silvery walls reduce heat loss by

(b)_____

hot (or cold) liquid

vacuum reduces heat loss by

(c)_____

q & a

Q. *Why am I told it's better to put on 'several layers' when it's cold outside?*

A. Each layer of clothing traps a layer of air between it and the next layer. Air is a good insulator.

Q. *How does double glazing work?*

A. In double glazing a layer of air is trapped between the two panes of glass. And as we have said, trapped air is a good insulator.

Q. *How much money could be saved if the walls and roof of a house were insulated effectively?*

A. Insulating the roof can reduce losses by up to 20%. Wall insulation can reduce losses by up to 35%. This could save more than 50% on your heating bill.

Question 5
An insulating jacket on a hot water tank could save £10-£15 a year.
(a) How is heat energy spread around the water in a hot water tank?
(b) How does heat energy escape from a hot water tank? And the answer isn't 'by turning the tap on!'

Answer

Unscramble these letters and put the words into pairs:

1. NOILSNUITA _____

2. VEONCCNOTI _____

3. POST GRAHATDS ____ _____

4. NRIAOTIDA _____

5. NOCCUDNTIO _____

6. SYNHI FURSCEA _____ _____

Number ____ goes with number ____

Number ____ goes with number ____

Number ____ goes with number ____

39

Physical science applications

Radiation and waves part 1

What's a wave?

A wave is moving energy, not material. Pull a rope tight, then move one end up and down, or side to side. A wave of energy travels along the rope. The rope itself doesn't travel. Similarly, ripples in a pond travel along, but the water itself only moves up and down. These are **transverse waves**. The wave's **peaks** and **troughs** travel along at right angles to the vibration.

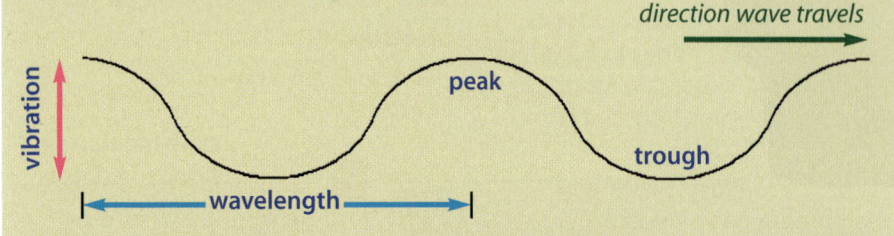

Alternately, push and pull one end of a *Slinky* spring. Pushing causes **compression**. Pulling causes **rarefaction**. Again, an energy wave travels along, but this time the coils of the spring move back and forth. This is a **longitudinal wave**. The wave travels in the same direction as the vibration.

Transverse waves	Longitudinal waves
water waves and ripples	sound waves
electromagnetic waves (light, radio, X-rays)	pressure (P) waves from earthquakes
vibrations in string instruments	vibrations in wind instruments

Distinguishing features of waves

Feature	What it means	Units
Speed, v	How fast the wave travels along. Depends on what the wave is travelling through.	metres per second (m s^{-1})
Wavelength, λ	Distance between two equivalent parts of the wave, e.g.: two peaks or troughs of a transverse wave; two areas of compression in a longitudinal wave.	metres (m)
Frequency, f	How many times a complete wave passes in 1 second. 1 hertz = 1 wave per second.	hertz (Hz)
Amplitude	Size of the vibration (up and down, or back and forth). Determines the brightness of light or loudness of sound.	

Wavelength and frequency are linked ...
The longer the wavelength, the lower the frequency. They determine the colour of visible light and the pitch of sound.

speed of wave = wavelength × frequency
$$v = f\lambda$$

Electromagnetic spectrum

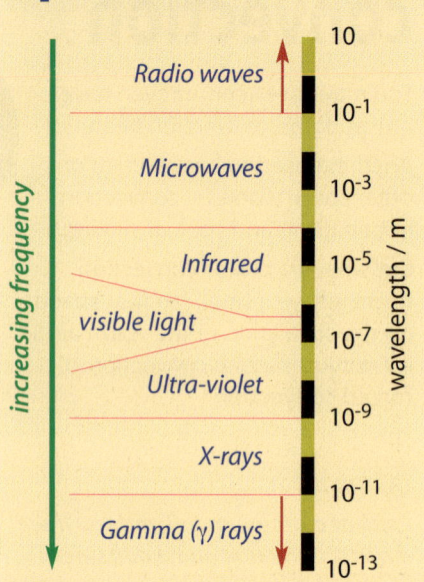

Radio waves — 10
Microwaves — 10^{-1}, 10^{-3}
Infrared — 10^{-5}
visible light — 10^{-7}
Ultra-violet — 10^{-9}
X-rays — 10^{-11}
Gamma (γ) rays — 10^{-13}

wavelength / m
increasing frequency

Visible light:
short — wavelength — long
high — frequency — low

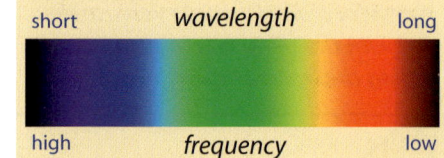

All electromagnetic waves travel at the same speed: 3×10^8 m s^{-1} in a vacuum, slightly slower through air, and slower still through other transparent materials.

Uses

Radio waves: radio and TV broadcasts; Wi-Fi computer equipment

Microwaves: telecommunications; radar; microwave cookers

Infrared: security light sensors; TV remote controls

visible light: seeing with eyes; photography

ultraviolet: tanning; treating jaundice in babies

X-rays and γ-rays: medical imaging (seeing inside the body)

The higher the frequency, the higher the **energy** of the wave.
Ultraviolet, X-rays and gamma rays are increasingly dangerous to living cells. For medical use, doses must be very small.

Reflection

Light beams travel in straight lines, but can bounce off things.

A light beam reflects off a flat surface at the same angle as it hits it.

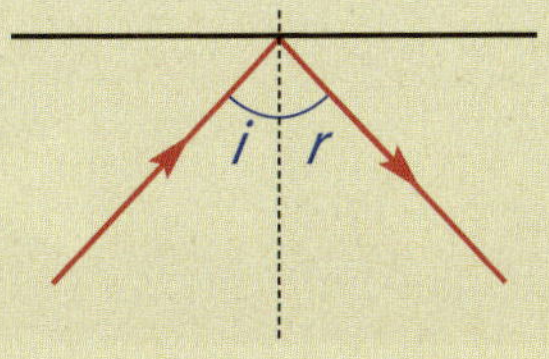

angle of incidence, *i* = angle of reflection, *r*

All visible materials reflect light. You can't see something unless light reflects from it into your eyes. If it reflects only part of the visible spectrum it appears coloured.

- Red objects reflect red light, and absorb all other wavelengths.
- White objects reflect all wavelengths.
- Black objects absorb all wavelengths and reflect no light. You can only see them against a lighter background.

Mirrors and periscopes rely on reflection.

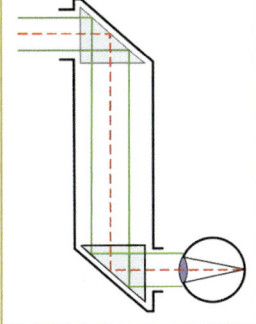

Far left: Australian sniper using a periscope rifle at Gallipoli, 1915

Left: How light reflects in a periscope with 45° prisms.

Refraction

Light *bends* when it passes from one transparent material into another, such as from air into glass and out again. This is **refraction**.

This is how lenses work. Their shape bends light the way we want it to go.

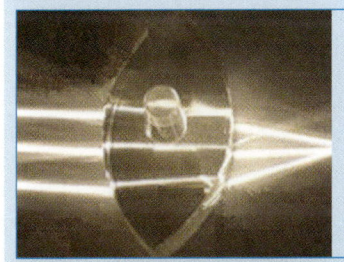

A convex lens bends light inwards. It makes the rays **converge**.

A concave lens bends light outwards. It makes the rays **diverge**.

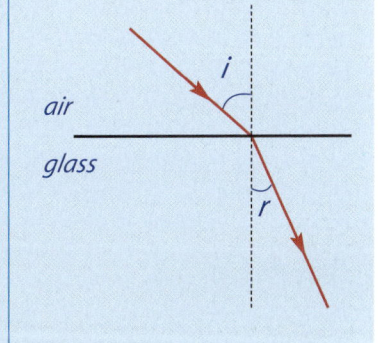

Unlike in reflection, angle of incidence, *i* **does not** equal angle of refraction, *r*.

The **refractive index** is given by

$$\frac{\sin i}{\sin r}$$

Photos reproduced under the terms of the GNU Free Documentation License

Eye lenses

Spectacle lenses are rigid. The lenses in your eyes can change shape, from strongly convex to slightly concave. This lets you focus far away or close to.

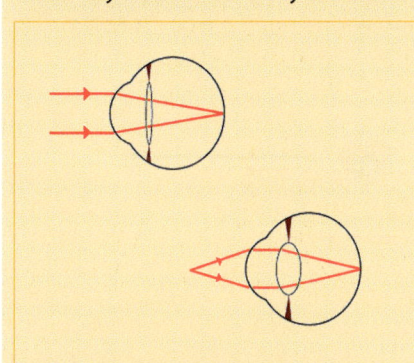

Light from a single point of a distant object (top) and light from a single point of a near object (bottom) brought into focus by changing the curvature of the lens.

If your eyes don't work properly, you need spectacles or contact lenses to help.

Short sighted people have eye lenses too convex - they focus in front of the retina.

So, they wear a **concave lens**.

Long sighted people have eye lenses that are not convex enough - they focus behind the retina.

So, they wear a **convex lens**.

Optical fibres

Periscopes work because the light reflects inside the triangular prisms. Internal reflection happens when the angle of incidence, *i*, is more than a certain size, (the critical angle). For glass, this is 41°.

Optical fibres work the same way. Light travels along inside the fibre, reflecting from side to side. Uses include:

- optical cables for telecommunications
- medical endoscopes for looking inside people.

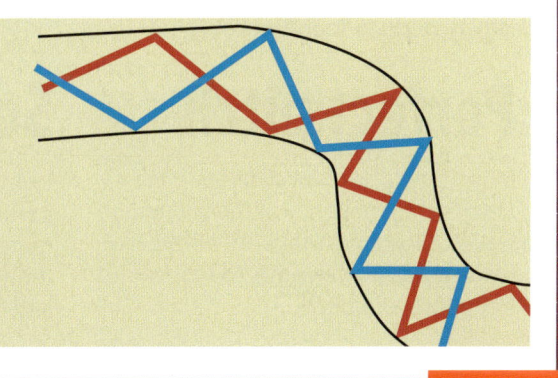

41

Physical science applications

Radiation and waves part 2

Ionising radiations

Radioactive substances emit three types of radiation. They're dangerous because they ionise molecules in living cells. This makes them perform the wrong biochemical reactions, damaging or killing the cells, or causing cancer.

alpha (α–) rays
- Stream of tiny particles, each made of two protons and two neutrons
- α–particles have a 2+ charge
- Stopped by a few centimetres of air, one sheet of paper, thin aluminium or lead foil

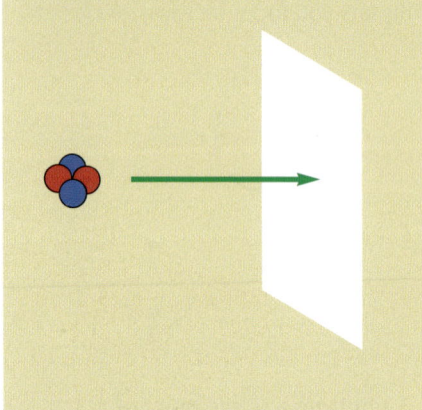

beta (β–) rays
- Stream of high speed electrons.
- β–particles have a 1– charge
- Pass through 5-10 metres of air
- Stopped by 50-100 sheets of paper, 2-4 mm aluminium or 1 mm of lead

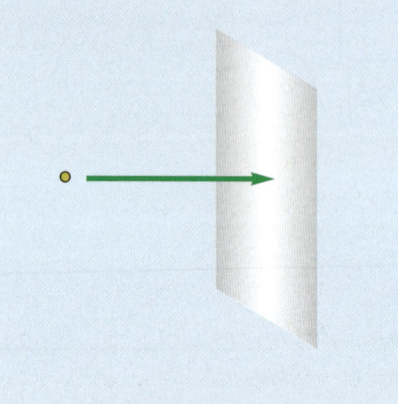

gamma (γ–) rays
- A form of electromagnetic radiation
- γ–rays have no charge
- Not absorbed by materials, but its energy decreases when it passes through. You need at least 10 cm of lead, or many metres of concrete, to reduce its energy to a safe level

Musical notes

Musical instruments produce sound by vibrating in different ways.

For example:
- We hit, pluck or stroke stringed instruments, such as pianos, guitars and violins.
  The strings vibrate, creating transverse waves.
- We blow wind instruments, such as trumpets.
  Air in a tube vibrates creating longitudinal waves.

These vibrations make the air vibrate. This causes changes in air pressure, which produce sound waves.

Vibrating strings
long wave = low pitch
finger shortening the string
shorter wave = higher pitch

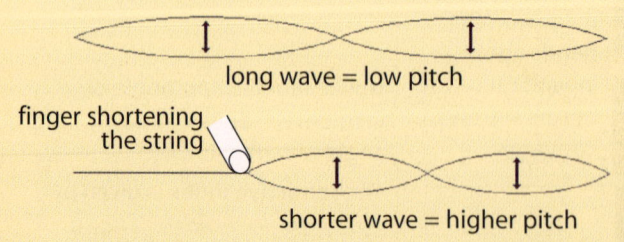

Air vibrating in a tube
blow
compression   rarefaction
shorter tube = higher pitch

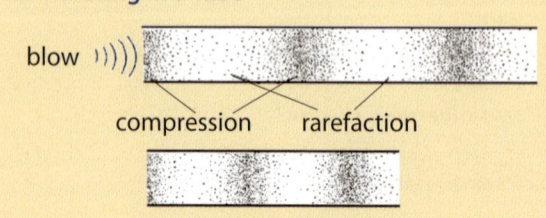

A tuba (top photo) has a lower pitch than a trumpet because it's longer.

Perfect pitch

Music needs notes of different pitch. Pitch is the frequency of the sound waves. Shorter instruments vibrate with shorter wavelength, so higher frequency and pitch.

Sound insulation

Light waves can travel through a vacuum. Sound waves cannot - they need particles to vibrate. Particles in solids and liquids are much closer together than in gases. Vibrations pass from one particle to the next more easily. So sound travels through solids and liquids better than through the air. That's why double glazing and foam are good sound insulators.

Communicating with waves

Someone shouts to you and waves. You see them via light waves and hear via sound waves. Speech and vision are our main forms of communication. But we can't see or hear things far away. We use other waves to help us - all the longer waves in the electromagnetic spectrum, from visible light up to radio waves.

Visible light allows us to read written communications. (You can't read in the dark.) It also delivers messages in other ways:

- **colour coding**, as in traffic lights, the flavours of sweets or values of resistors
- **flashing**, as in lighthouses or Morse code
- **shapes**, as in digital read-outs, or patterns of dots on a TV screen

Visible light only works along a **line-of-sight**. When we can't see the other person, we use another method.

Carrier waves

Postal systems carry written messages from place to place. Alternatively, you can turn messages into electrical signals and let waves carry them. That's how telephones, radio and TV work.

- **Camera and microphone turn sights and sounds into electrical signals**
- **Signals are coded onto a carrier wave**
- **Transmitter sends waves along cables or through the air**
- **Receiver detects waves and decodes signals**
- **Screen and loudspeaker reproduce the original sights and sounds**

We use electromagnetic waves as carriers. Longer wavelengths are better for carrying messages long distances.

Infrared

(wavelength = 10^{-6} to 10^{-3} m)

Carries coded instructions from a remote control handset to a TV, video or hi-fi. The light carrying messages along optical fibres is also usually infrared.

Microwaves

(wavelength = 10^{-3} to 10^{-1} m)

Carry telecommunications, such as mobile phone signals, across the network of masts and aerials. Fixed (land-line) telephone messages use microwave links between cities.

Microwaves also carry signals to and from satellites for international telecommunications and TV broadcasts.

Radio waves

(wavelength = 10^{-1} to 10^{4} m)

Carry terrestrial radio and TV broadcast signals. The wide range of wavelengths is split into five **bands**: Short, Medium and Long Wave radio, plus VHF (very high frequency) for FM radio, and UHF (ultra high frequency) for TV broadcasts.

Remember the link between wavelength and frequency. Do VHF and UHF use shorter or longer wavelengths than the other three radio bands?

Coding the signals

To carry messages, we modulate the carrier wave by combining it with the electrical signal.

The receiver later separates it out again. There are three methods:

- frequency modulation (FM) codes the signal by varying the frequency of the carrier wave
- amplitude modulation (AM) varies the amplitude instead
- pulse code modulation (PCM) produces a digital signal - a string of *ons* and *offs*.

Physical science applications

Fossil fuels

Fossil fuels supply meet most of energy demands.
But their use has also caused environmental problems such as global warming.

What is a fuel?

A **fuel** is an **energy resource**. Food is a fuel. It provides us with energy to keep alive. Other fuels provide energy to power machines to:
- make things
- move things
- heat things
- light things
- generate electricity, which is used to power other machines.

It would be a mistake to take all this for granted. Fuels are non-renewable (or 'finite').

Question 1
What does 'fuels are non-renewable' mean?

Answer

What is a fossil fuel?

Coal, oil and **natural gas** are fossil fuels. They are stores of energy. In the UK these fossil fuels provide the following percentages of our energy needs:

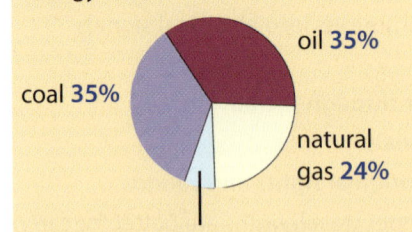

- oil 35%
- coal 35%
- natural gas 24%

The remaining 6% or so comes from alternative energy resources.

When fossil fuels are burned heat energy is released.

fossil fuel + oxygen →
carbon dioxide + water + **heat energy**

The carbon dioxide formed can cause environmental problems.

Question 2
What elements are fossil fuels made from?

Answer

Mining and drilling

Fossil fuels began as living things. Millions of years ago trees and other organisms died. They decayed. Layer upon layer were squashed under stronger and stronger pressures. The result? **Fossil fuels** (**coal, oil** and **natural gas**) buried beneath the earth's surface.

Coal is mined. Oil and gas are drilled for. In the UK oil and gas come from beneath the sea bed. They have to be piped to where they are going to be used.

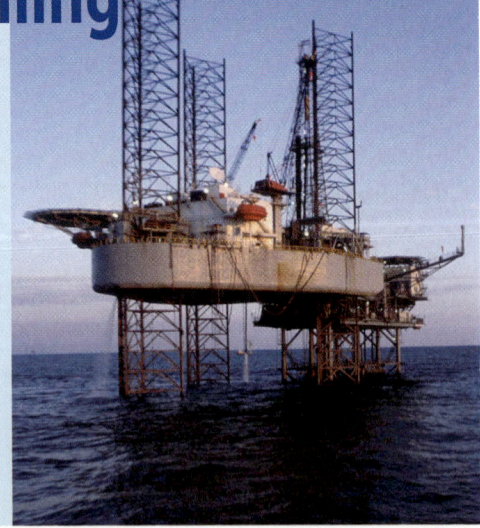

A burning problem

Limited deposits

- Energy cannot be destroyed, but energy resources can. *Remember: 'Fossil fuels are finite'* - when they're gone, they're gone. We can't make more.
- Fossil fuels, particularly oil, are our main source of organic chemicals. If we burn them all, there'll be none left to make medicines, plastics, dyes, paints, detergents, etc.

Question 3
Which fossil fuel is a solid and which is a liquid?

Answer

Did you know?

In the United States of America oil is nicknamed 'black gold' because it's so valuable.

Pollution

Fossil fuels are not the only cause of pollution. Domestic waste and waste from industry and agriculture can cause problems if they're not disposed of carefully.

There are options:

- **incineration**
  burning the waste, but this can also result in air pollution
- **land-fill**
  burying the waste, but hazardous substances might be washed out by rain into rivers and lakes
  (the main crticism of land-fill is the amount of land it takes)
- **recycling**
  however, this often requires energy and, therefore, burning more fossil fuels.

Pollution indicators

Chemical tests can be carried out. For example, checking the quality of water in rivers and lakes by:

- measuring pH
- determining concentrations of ammonia, nitrate, phosphate and metal ions.

Living organisms also indicate pollution. The Environment Agency uses a number of indicator species to monitor pollution.

Global warming

- Burning fossil fuels releases carbon dioxide into the atmosphere.
- Carbon dioxide is a greenhouse gas. It reduces the amount of heat radiated from the earth into space.
- This raises the temperature of the atmosphere.
- This global warming affects climate and weather. It may melt the polar ice caps causing sea levels to rise.

Air pollution

Burning fossil fuels also produces sulfur dioxide, which causes acid rain and damages people's lungs. This problem is reduced by:

- removing sulfur compounds from natural gas before distributing it to customers
- using limestone to absorb sulfur dioxide from chimney gases at some power stations
- fitting catalytic converters that tackle pollutants in vehicle exhausts.

Renewable and non-renewable resources

Renewable resources
- everlasting supply of energy
- will not run out

Non-renewable resources
- once used they can't be replaced
- they will eventually run out

Biofuels
- wood
- straw
- plants
(of course, these would run out if we didn't keep growing them)

Sun
- solar energy

Water
- hydroelectric power (HEP)
- waves
- tides

Wind

Fossil fuels
- coal
- oil
- natural gas

Nuclear fuels

Primary and secondary resources

Fuels are **primary energy resources**. They are the starting point for energy production. Burning fuels can be used to change their stored energy into, for example, electricity (a **secondary energy resource**).

Question 4
Why does burning biofuels produce carbon dioxide?

Answer

Question 5
Write down three problems caused by burning fossil fuels to release energy.

Answer

Find ten words related to fossil fuels. The first one's been done for you.

```
      C G O
      A L N
    G R O A E
    R B B T T
  W E O A U I Q
  T A E N L R N S C
  A T N D W A I F O
  E E H I A L F U A
  H R O O R G L E L
  K U X M A Y L
      S I I S O
      E D N L A
        E G A
        O I L
```

45

Physical science applications

Alternative energy resources

Fossil fuels are finite. They will not last for ever.
Consequently we are constantly searching for alternative resources of energy.

Alternative to what?

Fossil fuels provide us with around 94% of our energy needs. However, as explained on the previous page, there are problems: limited supplies, global warming and pollution. Alternatives to fossil fuels include:

- nuclear
- wind
- solar
- hydroelectric
- wave
- tidal

The nuclear alternative

Uranium is a fuel. One kilogram stores the same amount of energy as one million kilograms of coal. Unlike fossil fuels uranium isn't burned.

Uranium is made up of:
- 99.3% uranium-238. This is stable and doesn't release energy;
- 0.7% uranium-235. This is unstable and is the source of energy.

Atoms of uranium-235 split into two, releasing energy. This is called nuclear fission. About 17% of the world's electricity comes from nuclear energy.

Question 1
What does fission mean? Answer

Problems with nuclear

No harmful gases are given off when nuclear energy is used. However, there are problems ...

Radioactive emissions

Nuclear fission produces radioactive emissions (sometimes called radiation) as well as energy. They are extremely dangerous to living organisms, damaging or even killing cells.

Large scale problems in nuclear reactors are extremely rare, but they do occur. One example is the accident at the nuclear power station in Chernobyl in the former USSR in 1986. Mikhail Gorbachev, who was Soviet president at the time, made this address:

"Good evening comrades. All of you know that there has been an incredible misfortune - the accident at the Chernobyl nuclear plant. It has painfully affected the Soviet people and shocked the international community. For the first time we confront the real force of nuclear energy out of control."

Nuclear waste

After use, nuclear fuels become 'spent'. The spent fuel is radioactive. People handling it must be protected. The spent fuel is stored in special containers. These stop the radiation from escaping and are strong so that they don't break in case of an accident.

Nuclear energy: pros and cons

Fill in the gaps ...

Pros

A Enormous amounts of _____ from small amounts of fuel.

B No _____ and so no carbon dioxide or sulfur dioxide released.

C _____ resource, but enough to last for thousands of years.

Cons

D Materials emit very dangerous _____ and so need to be carefully controlled.

E Handling the materials is _____.

F Nuclear _____ is unlikely, but possible.

G Radioactive _____ from nuclear power stations must be stored for centuries, but people can't agree on how or where.

Water-balanced railway

Here is an unusual way to use the energy of moving water.

At the centre for Alternative Technology in mid-Wales, they've built a railway on a cliff. It's called a water-balanced railway. Two trains are used. As one goes down, the other goes up.

Where does the energy come from? A tank in the train at the top is filled with water from a lake.

This makes it heavier than the train at the bottom. It travels down, lifting the other train up.

When it gets to the bottom, its tank of water is emptied.

The train at the top now gets its tank filled with water ... and so on.

Find five alternative energy resources:

N	W	W	W	N	H	F	A	V	S
D	N	A	K	U	V	A	L	O	D
P	I	X	H	C	X	P	L	O	N
L	H	D	W	L	C	A	N	W	I
M	D	A	C	E	R	H	J	I	W
L	V	T	G	A	E	L	M	I	T
E	J	A	S	R	T	I	D	A	L
G	E	Z	T	E	A	M	O	D	F
W	J	Y	T	M	G	Y	C	E	D
T	B	K	G	J	E	M	O	U	K

Renewable energy resources

Unlike fossil fuels or nuclear fuel, these supplies will always be available.

Question 2
What's wrong with the statement 'we produce energy'?

> Answer

Wind
- Moving air has kinetic energy.
- Wind turbines change this into electrical energy by turning a generator.

Question 3
What is a wind farm?

> Answer

Solar
The Sun gives us heat and light.
- Solar panels collect heat, providing hot water.
- Solar cells change light energy directly into electrical energy. *Beware! A collection of solar cells is sometimes called a solar panel.*

Water power
Moving water has kinetic energy. This can be changed into electrical energy.
- Wave energy - the rise and fall of waves is converted into rotary movement. This turns turbines, generating electricity.
- Water running in a river - often held back by dams and released to give a big flow. This produces **hydroelectric power**.
- The tide coming in and going out - **tidal** turbines change this into electrical energy.

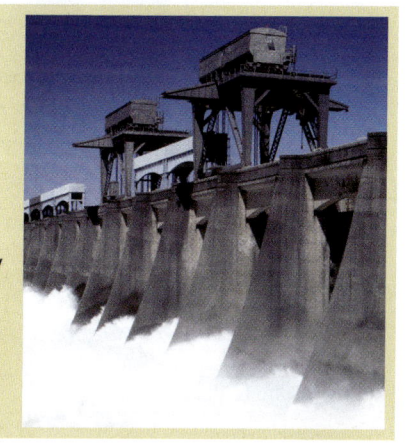

Problems with renewable energy

Reliability
The weather in the UK is unpredictable. The sun doesn't always shine and the wind doesn't always blow. Solar, wind and hydroelectric power depend on the weather, so they can be unreliable.

Effects of the environment
- Wildlife and wildlife habitats might be harmed (for example, by tidal barrages).
- Often unsightly and sometimes noisy (for example, wind farms).

Question 4
What is a 'wildlife habitat'?

> Answer

Did you know?
In less than one hour as much solar energy arrives on the planet as the entire world population uses in one year!

47

Physical science applications

Generating electricity

Electricity is generated in power stations. Energy, e.g. chemical energy in fossil fuels, is transformed to electricity. This is distributed through the National Grid.

Making it and getting it

Electricity has to be **generated**. This means changing energy in one form, for example chemical energy, into electrical energy. The chemical energy locked up in fossil fuels is changed into electrical energy in **power stations**. But that's just the first part of the job. Once generated, the electricity must be taken to where it's needed - factories, offices, houses, hospitals and so on. This is done through the **National Grid**.

Releasing locked up energy

Fossil fuels (**coal**, **oil** and **natural gas**) are primary resources of energy. It is stored as chemical energy. In a power station this chemical energy is changed into electrical energy. Here is an energy transfer diagram for a power station:

energy input → chemical energy

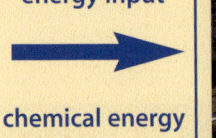

energy output → electrical energy

Transfer takes place in the power station

The diagram simplifies the processes. So, what's going on in the power station?

- When fossil fuels are burned their chemical energy is changed into **heat energy**. Carbon dioxide and water (in the form of steam) are made.

Question 1
Write a word equation to represent the reaction when a fossil fuel is burned.

Answer

- This heat is used in power stations to boil water and produce **steam**.
- Further heating increases the steam's pressure.
- High pressure steam turns the blades of **steam turbines**. This is similar to the wind turning the sails of a windmill. The turbine blades turn at high speeds.
- The blades are attached to a shaft which also turns.
- The turbine shaft turns the electricity generator.
- This produces **electricity**.

Question 2
What form of energy is there in:
(a) a fossil fuel
(b) a spinning turbine blade?

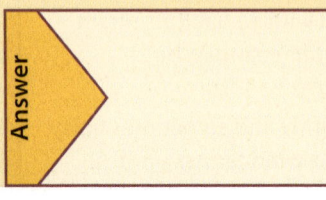

Answer

---

fossil fuels are burned to heat water and make steam

↓

fossil fuels heat the steam more until it's very hot

Chemical energy changes into heat energy

↓

the steam is released into a turbine

↓

the force of the steam makes the blades turn

Heat energy changes into kinetic energy

↓

the turbine shaft drives the generator

↓

electricity is generated

Kinetic energy changes into electrical energy.

↓

electricity is distributed via the National Grid

← steam condenses (forms water) and is fed back to the boiler

48

The generator

With the exception of solar power, turbines are the key to electricity generation.

Whether by wind or running water, turbine blades are made to turn.

- These turbines are linked to a coil of metal wire.
- Their movement causes the coil to rotate.
- The coil is in a large magnet.
- As the coil of wire spins in the magnet an electric current is produced.

Power station efficiency

Power stations aren't very efficient. Only one-third of a fossil fuel's chemical energy is changed into electrical energy. The rest is wasted, mainly as heat.

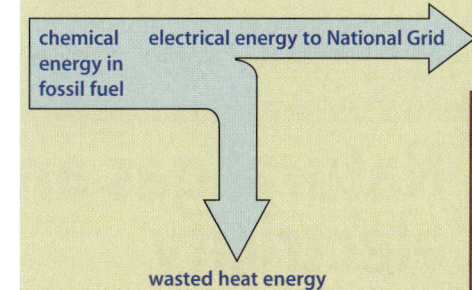

chemical energy in fossil fuel → electrical energy to National Grid → wasted heat energy

Question 3

(a) What happens to the carbon dioxide that's produced?

(b) What law tells you that the chemical energy in the fossil fuel equals the sum of the electrical energy and heat energy produced in a power station?

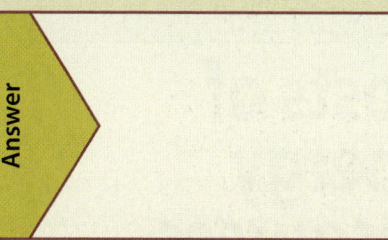

Answer

q & a

Q. What fossil fuels are used in power stations?

A. Coal and natural gas. Only small amounts of oil are used. The relative amount of coal, gas and oil vary. For example:

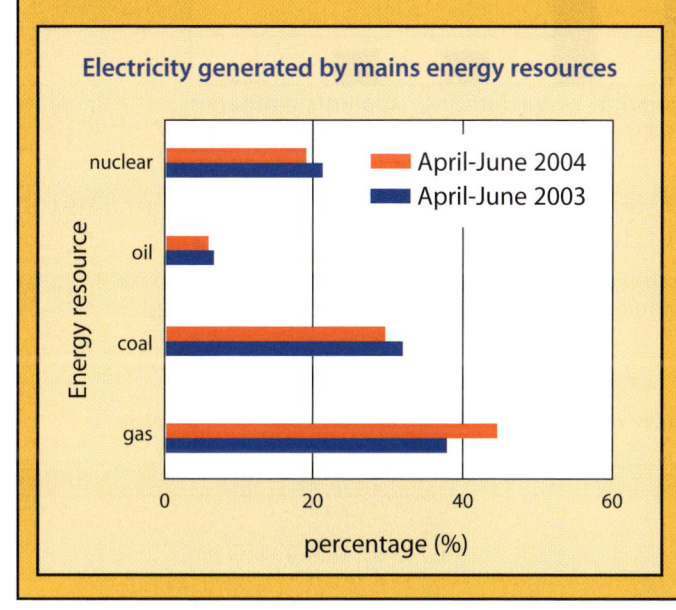

Electricity generated by mains energy resources

(Bar chart showing April–June 2004 and April–June 2003 percentages for nuclear, oil, coal, and gas)

Q. How much energy does a power station produce?

A. Of course it varies from power station to power station. Longannet power station in Scotland is the second largest coal-fired power station in the UK. It's capable of producing 10,000,000,000 kilowatt hours of electrical energy each year - enough to meet the needs of two-million people.

Q. What is 'the National Grid'?

A. It's the network of cables carrying electricity from the power stations to homes, offices, factories and other places where it's needed. It consists of 4,500 miles of high-voltage overhead line and 400 miles of underground cable. The electricity transmitted across England and Wales each year is equivalent to the energy needed to put 100,000 space shuttles into orbit.

Q. Does all the electricity distributed through the National Grid come from fossil fuel power stations?

A. No. Nuclear fuel makes up about 20-25% of the energy resources used to generate electricity.

Complete this crossword:

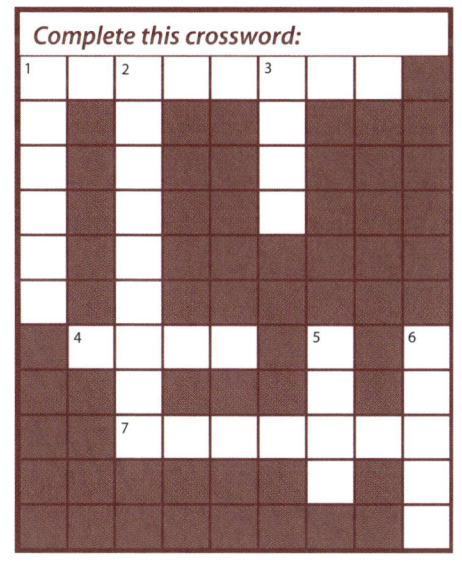

Question 4

Why does the output from a power station depend on the time of year?

Answer

Crossword clues

Across:

1. _ _ _ _ _ _ energy is stored in a fossil fuel.
4. _ _ _ _ energy is produced when a fossil fuel burns.
7. A _ _ _ _ _ _ _ shaft turns the electricity generator.

Down:

1. _ _ _ _ _ _ dioxide is formed when fossil fuels are burned.
2. Wasted heat energy means power stations are not very _ _ _ _ _ _ _ _ _.
3. _ _ _ _ is a fossil fuel burned in many power stations.
5. Electricity is distributed through the National _ _ _ _.
6. Makes the turbine blades turn.

49

Physical science applications

Choosing and using energy resources

Often you have a choice of energy resources. For example, a lawnmower might have an electrical motor or a petrol motor, or it might simply be pushed by hand.

Costs of energy resources

Important energy resources include:

- natural gas
- mains electricity
- batteries

Energy companies are competitive. Prices for the same amount of gas or electricity vary. For example, a quick internet search showed that the same amount of electricity could be bought from 20 companies at prices from £890 to £1080.

q & a

Q. *If electricity costs so much more than gas, why should I even bother with electricity?*

A. Not everything runs off gas (for example, televisions and computers). Gas is good for cooking and heating, but not much else. When you do have a choice between gas and electricity there are other things to think about. For example, if you have the choice between a gas cooker and an electric cooker:

- what do they cost to buy
- what does it cost to have then serviced?

Natural gas and mains electricity

In our houses we use energy for heat, light, sound and to make machines work.

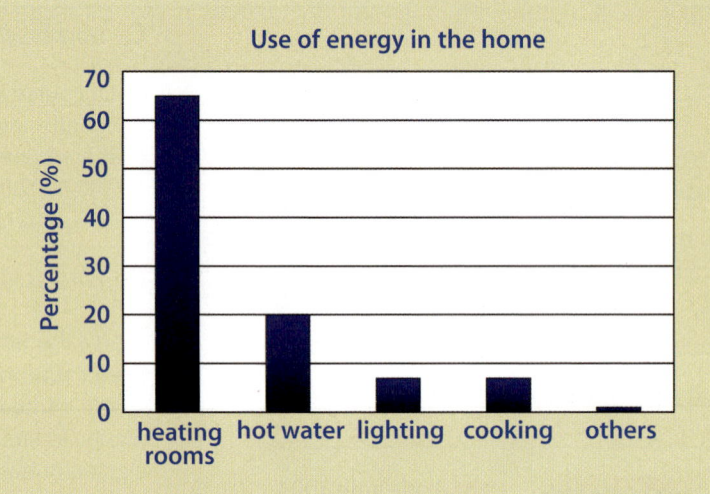

Use of energy in the home

(Bar chart showing Percentage (%) vs categories: heating rooms ~65%, hot water ~20%, lighting ~7%, cooking ~7%, others ~1%)

Factories, hospitals, schools, sports stadiums, cinemas, theatres and other places of work and leisure also use large amounts of energy.

The most common resources of energy for these places are natural gas and electricity. However, sometimes other fossil fuels or biofuels are burned to provide heat.

Question 1
(a) What fossil fuels other than natural gas can be burned to heat a house?
(b) What is the main biofuel burned to heat a house?

Answer

Natural gas is methane, with small amounts of impurities. In the home, energy from gas costs about 1.7 p per kilowatt hour.

95% of our mains electricity is generated from coal, gas and nuclear fuels. In the home, electrical energy costs about 6.5 p per kilowatt hour.

Question 2
How many times more expensive is mains electricity than natural gas?

Answer

Did you know?

Car batteries (12 V) are recharged when the car's engine is running.

Industrial applications

Industry is a huge consumer of electrical energy. The electrical energy is transformed into other forms for:

Movement: goods, people

Heating: buildings, reaction mixtures, processing materials

Lighting: buildings and outdoor areas that need to be lit at night, screens and other displays

Sound: telephones, bells, buzzers, PA systems

Find two types of battery and three ways energy may be provided in the laboratory ...

```
      E G
    N H L N Z Y
    A G B Y G C
X M T N A R N O I B
T A U I E E I O V U
P I R T G T T K U T
M N A H R T A I V T
O S L G A A E N J O
S M G I H B H G T N
    A L C F T T
    S H E H O D
        R N
```

Batteries

In a cell, chemical energy is changed into electrical energy. Batteries are made of two or more cells, connected end-to-end.

Some devices only work off batteries. Others can be powered using either mains electricity or batteries. They are convenient, but the electricity is more expensive than mains electricity.

Conventional batteries

- Usually 1.5 V cells, or 3 V, 6 V or 9 V batteries
- Used in torches and toys
- Cheapest type of battery

Button batteries

- 1.4 V, 1.55 V and 3 V cells
- Used in calculators and wrist watches
- Expensive, but very small / slimline

Rechargeable batteries

- 1.2 V and 4 V
- Used in laptops, power tools and mobile phones
- Expensive but can be recharged hundreds of times

Note: conventional batteries can be replaced by small rechargeable batteries.

Question 3

(a) What type of battery would you use in (i) a watch (ii) hearing aid (iii) mobile phone (iv) television remote control?

(b) How many 1.5 V cells in (i) a 6 V battery (ii) a 9 V battery?

Answer

Matching the energy resource to the job

In the laboratory

The Bunsen burner, burning natural gas, is the traditional way of heating things in the laboratory. Just like cooking with gas, it's easy to control. However, many substances are flammable and could catch fire if heated with a naked flame.

Heating mantles, hot plates and water baths, powered by mains electricity, are good alternatives. Mains electricity is also used to power equipment such as lights, stirrers, pumps, electronic measuring instruments and computers.

Question 4

Which of these would you use to heat ethanol (a flammable liquid): Bunsen burner or electric hotplate?

Answer

In the field

Battery-powered equipment is vital for work in the field. After all, there's nowhere to plug in electrical instruments. Measurements can be made with battery-powered pH meters and colorimeters, and results recorded on a laptop computer. The batteries should be fully charged before starting work. Anything used in the field must be tough and robust.

Credit: Keith Weller, USDA

Question 5

Which types of scientists might use battery-powered equipment in the field?

Answer

Physical science applications

Counting the cost

Electricity isn't free. The amount you use depends on the power needed by an electrical appliance. The cost of running the appliance depends on the power it needs, how long it is used and the price of electricity.

Not all heat losses are unwanted

Often we insulate things to prevent heat losses. However, sometimes heat losses are needed. For example, heat energy transfer through:
- radiators in central heating systems
- a car radiator
- the cooling fins at the back of a fridge.

All of these are heat exchangers. They are designed to speed up heat transfer.

Question 1
What are the three ways heat energy can be transferred?

Answer

Heat exchangers

Heat exchangers may be used for heating or cooling. They are often pipes or tubes through which gases or liquids flow.

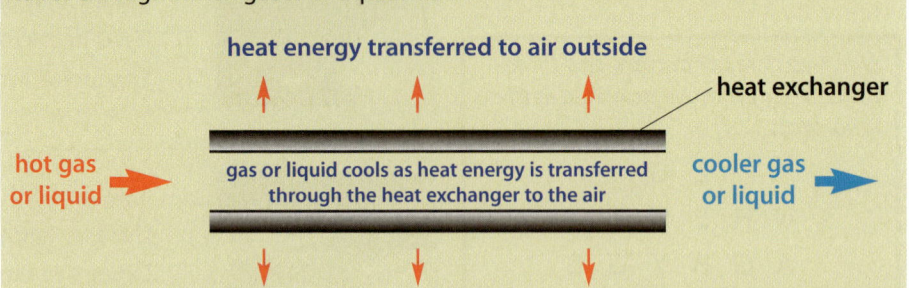

heat energy transferred to air outside

heat exchanger

hot gas or liquid → gas or liquid cools as heat energy is transferred through the heat exchanger to the air → cooler gas or liquid

A hot liquid or gas can be cooled by passing it through a heat exchanger surrounded by air. The air becomes hot. A liquid is sometimes used instead of air. Sometimes this heat energy is wasted. For example, in a car, heat energy is simply spread out into the air through the radiator. However, sometimes the idea is to warm the air in a confined space. For example, a heating radiator transfers heat energy to raise the temperature of a room.

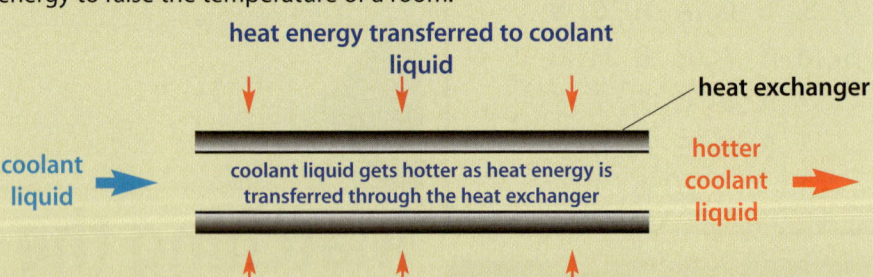

heat energy transferred to coolant liquid

heat exchanger

coolant liquid → coolant liquid gets hotter as heat energy is transferred through the heat exchanger → hotter coolant liquid

Heat exchangers are used to capture and recycle heat energy. Heat energy flows from something hot, such as a reaction vessel, to a coolant liquid. The heat energy is carried by the liquid to where it's needed. It could be used to heat another liquid or gas used in the process. The nuclear power station described on the next page is an example.

Question 2
Why is the coolant a liquid rather than a gas?

Answer

Surface area and thickness

- Heat exchangers should have a **large surface area** to increase the contact between hot and cold. Look at the design of a heating radiator or the fins on the back of a fridge.
- They should have **thin** walls to increase the rate of heat transfer, but still strong enough not to break.

What are they made of?

Heat exchangers are made of materials that **conduct heat energy well**. Metals are excellent.

Unscramble the names of the ten materials (right).

Good for making heat exchangers:

LUUIMMNIA _____

POPREC _____

HITGRAPE _____

ORNI _____

LESTE _____

Not good for making heat exchangers:

RODRABACD _____

CRACIME _____

STALICP _____

BURBRE _____

DOWO _____

52

The cost of industrial power

Industry needs power to make things work ... and it needs lots of it.

In particular, manufacturing industries need to heat and move heavy things.

The energy comes from the National Grid or gas piped into the site.

Many industries have their own generators, often for use in case of emergency, e.g. a power cut.

They pay a different rate to the domestic consumer, but the principle is the same.

The other cost of industrial power is the damage heavy energy use might have on our environment.

Industry is aware of the problem and does much to limit potential damage.

Most companies have a policy on sustainability.

Heat exchangers in power stations

Heat energy is produced in power stations from nuclear fuels or fossil fuels. The steam drives a turbine. The turbine, in turn, generates electricity.

The diagram shows how electricity is generated from nuclear fuel.

- The fuel rods get hot.
- The fuel rods heat the coolant liquid.
- The hot coolant liquid is passed through a heat exchanger in a boiler.
- Heat energy is transferred to the water via the heat exchanger.
- The water in the boiler boils to form steam.

A second heat exchanger uses water from a reservoir to condense steam after it has passed through the turbine. The water that forms is sent back into the boiler.

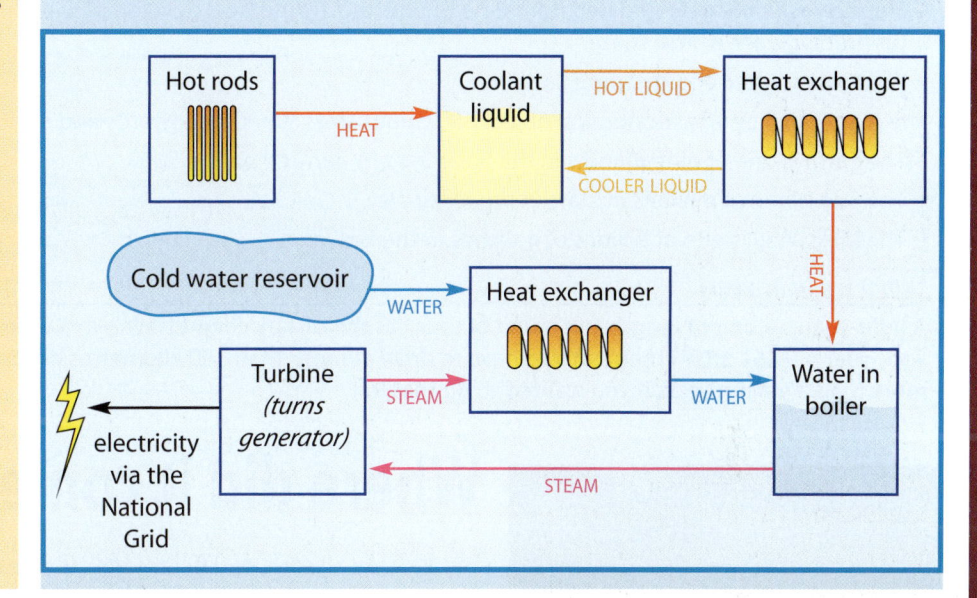

Keeping cool

Heat exchangers are used extensively in the chemical industry. Many reactions used to make chemicals are exothermic. In other words, they give out heat energy. And as you know, the hotter a reaction gets, the faster it goes. This means some exothermic reactions could get out of control. The safe solution is to cool them down using a heat exchanger. It's safe *and* the captured energy can be recycled.

Question 3
How does a distillation condenser act as a heat exchanger?

Answer

What makes the best coolant?

Two factors to consider:
- the heat capacity
- the cost.

The effectiveness of a coolant depends on its specific heat capacity.

Specific heat capacity = heat energy needed to heat 1 g by 1 °C.

The more energy needed, the more effective the coolant.

Water is often used. It takes 4.18 joules to raise the temperature of 1 g of water by 1 °C. Water freezes below 0 °C, so antifreeze is added in car cooling systems.

Antifreeze is ethylene glycol. It takes 2.42 joules to raise the temperature of 1 g of it by 1 °C. Water is the better coolant, so just enough antifreeze is added to prevent the water from freezing.

Question 4
How many joules of energy are needed to raise the temperature of (a) 50 g water, and (b) 100 g ethylene glycol each by 5 °C?

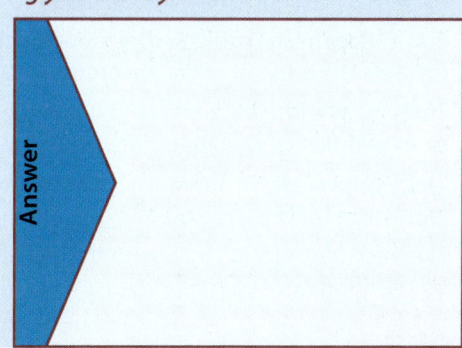

Answer

53

Physical science applications

The Universe part 1

What is the Universe?

In a word ... everything! Everything we can see, on Earth and out in space, and an awful lot more that we can't see.

Size: about 156 billion light-years* across, or 1.5 billion billion billion metres (1.5×10^{24} m)

This *best estimate* gets updated from time to time as astronomers develop new techniques for probing further into space.

Contents: matter, energy, space and time.

The matter makes up astronomical objects of various sizes. Working upwards and outwards:
- The Earth is one of nine **planets** in the Solar System, centred on the Sun.
- The Sun is one of millions of **stars** in the Milky Way.
- The Milky Way is one of billions of **galaxies** in the Universe.

What is a light-year?

A light-year is a unit of **length**, not a unit of time. It's the distance light travels in a year. One light-year = 9.461×10^{15} metres. You'd have to drive at more than 100 kilometres per hour for more than a million years if you wanted to go that far!

Where did it come from?

People have all sorts of different beliefs about how the Universe was created.

One popular theory among astronomers is **The Big Bang**.
- At the beginning of time, something smaller than an atom suddenly expanded.
- The Big Bang created matter and scattered it outwards.
- This matter formed protons, neutrons and electrons, which combined into small atoms, like hydrogen and helium.
- These fused into larger atoms.
- Gravity gradually pulled them together to make galaxies of stars.
- Some of the gases condensed into solid objects, like planets and comets.

All this took millions of years, and the process continues.
- Nuclear fusion of small atoms into larger ones is what powers the Sun and all other stars.
- Some 15 billion years later the Universe is still expanding.

How do we know?

Nuclear fusion in stars generates light.

Starlight and sunlight have similar **spectra**, because the same process produces the light.

But ... lines in starlight spectra show **redshift** - the lines are shifted towards the red end of the spectrum.

Their wavelength increases, and frequency decreases - just like the pitch of an ambulance siren as it goes past.

This **Doppler effect** shows that stars are moving away from us. In other words, the Universe is expanding.

Evidence for the size and age of the Universe comes from investigations by astronomers.

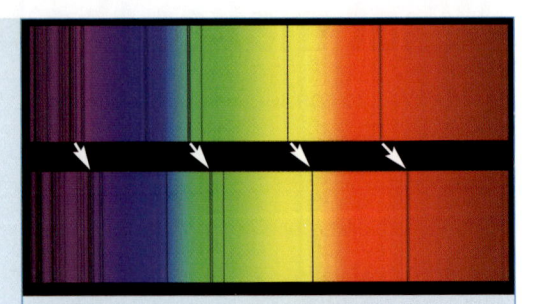

Redshift of spectral lines of a supercluster of distant galaxies (bottom), compared with the Sun (top), which is closer to earth.

How do we study the Universe?

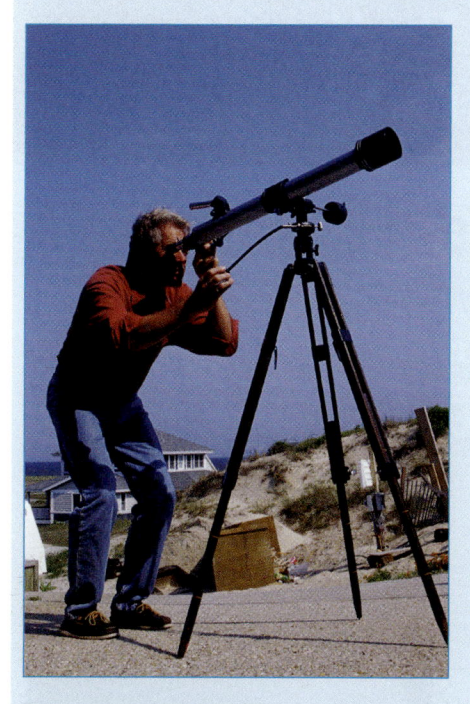

To see things far away, we need telescopes. Optical telescopes are the ones we look through or use to take photographs.

Problems

Clouds get in the way, and air pollution makes the view hazy.

Light pollution from streetlights blots out weaker stars - in the same way as sunlight prevents us seeing stars during the day.

Changes in air temperature bend light - like mirages in the desert.

Solutions

Build observatories on mountain tops, away from built-up areas.

Put telescopes in space, like the Hubble Space Telescope (HST) - very effective, but very expensive.

Types of telescope

Reflecting (uses mirrors)

Light enters through the open end and **reflects** off a concave mirror. It converges onto a flat mirror and reflects to form an image at the focal point. The eyepiece magnifies this image.

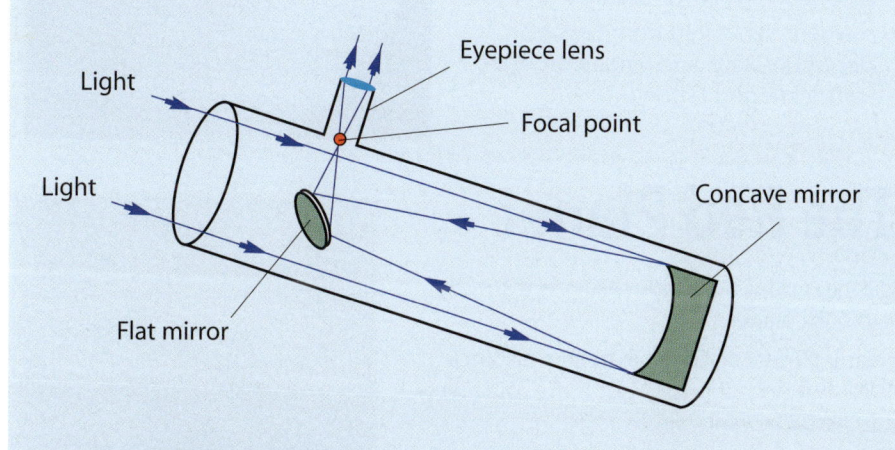

Refracting (uses lenses)

Light enters through the open end. An objective lens **refracts** the light and produces an image at the focal point. The eyepiece magnifies this image.

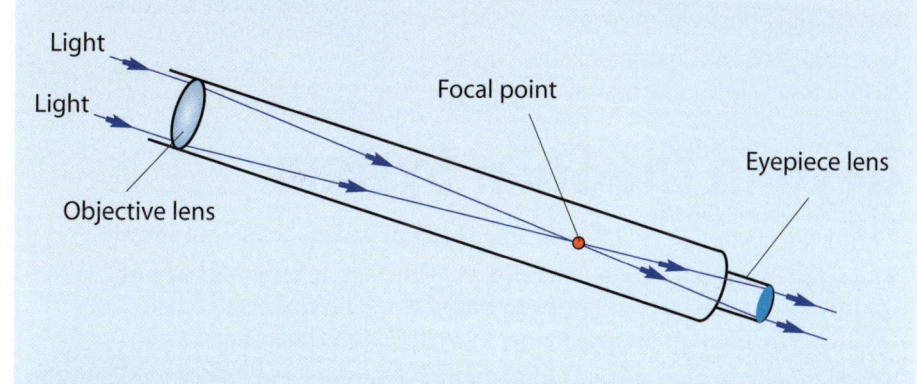

Electronic sensors

Modern telescopes use electronic sensors (similar to those in digital cameras) to collect the image, rather than the astronomer's eye.

Optical and other telescopes

Optical telescopes are limited. Visible light is only a small part of the electromagnetic spectrum. Astronomers gather information from other wavelengths too.

- Radio telescopes collect radio waves from objects that are not hot enough to give off visible light. These objects are therefore invisible to optical telescopes.

The Parkes radio telescope

- The Hubble Space Telescope (HST) detects infrared and ultraviolet as well as visible light.

HST

- X-ray and Gamma-ray telescopes only work in space, because the Earth's atmosphere absorbs these radiations. The instruments are mounted on satellites, such as the Chandra X-ray observatory. X-rays and gamma-rays are given off by extremely hot objects (above 1 million degrees), such as black holes.

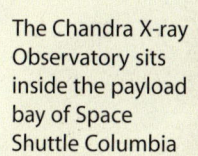

The Chandra X-ray Observatory sits inside the payload bay of Space Shuttle Columbia

Analytical chemists and forensic scientists use **spectroscopy** to decide which elements are in a sample. Similarly, astronomers study **spectra** of objects in space to find out what's in them. They can analyse radiation across the electromagnetic spectrum, not just coloured light.

55

Physical science applications

The Universe part 2

To boldly go ...

Space research involves going into space for a closer look - it's enormously expensive, but collects information that can't be obtained any other way.

Manned missions

Manned missions have so far been limited to Earth-orbit and the Moon, though exploration of Mars is being considered.

The Space Shuttle and Russian spacecraft are used for:
- research missions
- carrying satellites, such as the Chandra X-ray Observatory, into space
- ferrying parts and astronauts for the International Space Station (ISS).

Since 2000, there have always been at least two people in space, aboard the ISS. It is designed to have 10 main modules, and is still being built.

Space Shuttle docked onto the ISS

Unmanned space missions

Unmanned space missions investigate the whole Solar System (comets as well as planets).
- Fly-by spacecraft take photographs and collect data as they pass near the object - sometimes in orbit around it.
- Lander probes descend through the object's atmosphere (if any) and land on the surface. Instruments can then analyse actual samples.

Cassini-Huygens

The **Cassini-Huygens** mission, launched in 1997 combined both types.
- It performed fly-bys of Venus and Jupiter on its way to Saturn.
- It took detailed images of Jupiter's swirling clouds (photo, right).
- Cassini has been orbiting Saturn since 2004, investigating its rings and moons.
- It revealed at least three new moons.
- Huygens separated from Cassini in December 2005 and landed on Titan, Saturn's largest moon.

The Red Planet

Our next door neighbour, Mars, is the most explored planet.

Nearly 50 spacecraft have been sent since 1960, but only about 30 got there. The first successful landing was in 1971.

In 2006 four craft were orbiting Mars, including the European *Mars Express*. Two robot vehicles, *Spirit* and *Opportunity*, were exploring the surface, photographing the landscape and analysing samples. No evidence of life has been found - not even microbes.

Ten more Mars missions are planned up to 2016, possibly including manned flights.

The *Red* Planet is actually orangey-brown.

Credit: NASA, taken by *Spirit*.

Beyond the Solar System

Controlling spacecraft isn't like driving a car. You have to think well ahead ...

Radio signals take an hour to reach Cassini-Huygens at Saturn. So, when controllers send an instruction, it's an hour before the spacecraft receives it, and two hours before they know whether the instruction's been carried out.

Signals would take five times as long to reach Pluto. Beyond the Solar System, the nearest star is 4.3 light years away. Radio signals would take 4.3 years to reach it. Even travelling at 10 km s^{-1} (20 000 mph) a spacecraft would take more than 250 000 years. Such missions, even unmanned, are just science fiction. But then, so was any form of space ship 100 years ago.

Space spin-offs

Space research involves finding ways to do things that have never been attempted before. Scientists have to develop:
- new materials with special properties
- new technologies to achieve what was previously impossible.

These inventions soon find uses on earth. They become part of our everyday life.

New material or technology	Why it was developed	Public use
Ceramic foam insulation	Heat-resistant tiles to insulate the Space Shuttle during re-entry to the atmosphere	• Thermal and sound insulation in Boeing and Airbus planes • Thinner insulation gives more room inside fridges
Fire-resistant fabrics	For space suits	• Protective clothing for fire fighters
WD-40 	To prevent Atlas missiles rusting	• Aerosol for lubricating, de-rusting and removing water from metal parts
Satellites 	Military spying (USA v USSR)	• Telecommunications for international broadcasts and telephones • Remote monitoring of weather or pollution • Global positioning for *Sat-Nav* systems
Laser bar coding	To bar code Space Shuttle insulation tiles in a way that withstands the heat of re-entry	• Invisible, indestructible laser marking system can be used on almost anything, including farm animals
Robotics 	To perform mechanical tasks during unmanned space missions	• Mechanisation of boring, repetitive jobs • Dangerous work, such as bomb disposal or in radioactive areas
Infrared sensor	To measure temperature of distant stars	• Electronic thermometer - IR sensor measures body temperature when placed in the ear
Cordless power tools	So astronauts could do repairs in space	• Rechargeable, battery-powered hand tools
Joysticks 	For training astronauts to fly the Space Shuttle	• Computer game joysticks are modelled on Shuttle Simulator controls
Nutrition expertise	Good nutrition in pre-prepared meals for astronauts	• Better nutrition in pre-prepared meals for the elderly

Physical science applications

Sustainable Earth

Nature in the balance

Nature is very good at looking after itself. Natural problems usually have natural answers - but man-made problems don't. Man's activities have upset the balance of nature.

Problems include:
- increasing demands for energy
- decreasing finite resources - minerals and fossil fuels
- health and safety concerns - at work and to the public
- pollution - of air and water
- knock-on effects - global warming, the ozone hole, effects on wildlife.

How would we cope if the Sun didn't rise again?

The Energy problem

Energy cannot be created or destroyed. We can't make more, nor use it up. But ...
Using energy transforms it from one form into others - often including heat.
For example:

Process	Energy used	Energy produced
Burning fuels	Chemical	Heat
Exothermic reaction	Chemical	Heat
Electric lighting	Electrical	Light and heat
Electric motor	Electrical	Movement, sound and heat
Friction	Kinetic	Sound and heat

The problem is, heat escapes into the air and is lost. The energy is still there, but it's spread out. Like a car in bits, spread out energy is unusable. Unlike the car, we can't join energy together again.

The chemical industry tries to reduce these heat losses.

What industry can do	Example
Use energy sources that don't involve burning	extracting aluminium by electrolysis using hydroelectricity
Use processes that need less energy	catalysts and enzymes allow reactions to take place at lower temperatures
Recover waste heat	using heat exchangers, so heat given out can warm up in-coming reactants
Prevent heat escaping	insulating pipes and reactors, so less heat escapes to the air

© Norsk Hydro

A hydroelectric aluminium smelter in Norway.

Something to think about ...

Energy cannot be created. So how can some of it be renewable?

When it's gone, it's gone

We can't use up energy, but we can and do use up finite energy resources - mainly fossil fuels. Mineral resources are also finite and will run out sooner or later.

Problems

- Scientists expect oil and gas to run out within your lifetime.
- Burning fossil fuels leaves less to make petrochemicals, such as polymers and medicines.
- Unlike energy, there are no renewable mineral resources.
- Extracting minerals usually damages the landscape.

So, we need to limit our use of finite energy and mineral resources.

Solutions

Industry can:
- Make better use of energy.
- Increase use of alternative energy resources by developing renewable sources and nuclear power.
- Use raw materials more efficiently by (a) developing processes that give higher percentage yield, and (b) using reactions with high *atom economy*.
- Use materials more than once by (a) re-using products, such as glass bottles, and (b) recycling materials, such as metals, plastics and paper.

Health and safety matters

The Health and Safety at Work Act says employers must ensure the health, safety and welfare of employees while at work. The government's Health and Safety Executive checks that they do.

In addition, chemical industry associations around the world operate a *Responsible Care* programme. Member companies must protect the health and safety of all concerned.

Who's protected, and how?

Staff
Processes are operated safely, and hazards controlled. Workers follow safety rules.

Customers
Products are of suitable quality and *fit for purpose*. Hazard labels and instructions are clear.

General public
Consumer products meet the above requirements. Raw materials and products are transported safely.

The environment
Companies take steps to minimise damage caused by:
- extracting raw materials
- processing
- waste disposal.

Hazchem codes tell emergency services what to do if the tanker is in an accident.

Please dispose of carefully

Waste management should protect workers, the public and the environment.

It's easy to get rid of hazardous *products* - they are sold.

But hazardous *waste* can't just be thrown away - it must be disposed of safely. Options include:

- **recycling** - separating and reprocessing unreacted reactants
- **neutralising acids or alkalis** - provided the resulting salt is harmless
- **absorption** - for example, limestone absorbs sulfur dioxide from power station chimney gases
- **burial** - in disused mines, brine wells, and oil or gas wells
- **burning (incineration)** - mainly organic materials. This recovers some energy.

Nuclear waste is a major problem, because it will remain radioactive for thousands of years. So far there is no solution. Every suggestion raises major objections. Burial seems most likely, but everyone says NIMBY (Not In My Back Yard.)

Persistent problems

Some medicines work well, but have nasty side-effects. Similarly, some very useful chemicals turn out to have unwanted side-effects on the environment.

Persistent chemicals don't decompose away. They build up in the environment, increasing the problem.

Dichlorodiphenyltrichloroethane (DDT)

Use: insecticide - very effective against agricultural pests and malaria mosquitoes

Problem: DDT is a POP (Persistent Organic Pollutant).

It passes up the food chain. Tiny amounts in millions of insects build up to large amounts in birds of prey. It affects the birds' reproduction.

Use of DDT is now banned or restricted in many countries.

insect: tiny amount of DDT → **spider:** small amount of DDT → **small bird:** medium amount of DDT → **large bird of prey:** large amount of DDT

Chlorofluorocarbons (CFCs)

Use: aerosol propellant - very unreactive, so doesn't affect the aerosol contents.

Problem: CFCs attack the ozone layer, causing a large *hole*.

They rise into the upper atmosphere. Ultraviolet light sets off a chain reaction that decomposes ozone, O_3, into normal oxygen, O_2.

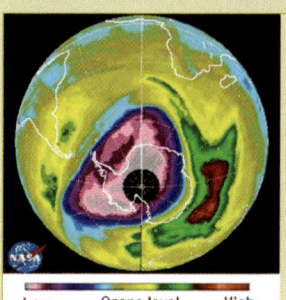

False-colour satellite image low levels of ozone over the Antarctic (the ozone *hole*).

Biological systems

Useful products from living organisms

Living organisms provide many useful things we use in everyday life. Scientists use their knowledge of biological systems to find the best ways to utilise this invaluable resource.

Animal, vegetable or mineral?

Think of all the things you use in everyday life. A few are natural, but most are man-made. Either way, they all come from:

living organisms

(plants, animals or micro-organisms)

non-living materials

(from the earth, sea or air).

You should be able to pick out, from a list, the products that have come from something living. For example:

Question 1

Which three of the following are obtained from living organisms?

lead • leather • penicillin
polyethene • salt • wool

1 _____

2 _____

3 _____

You also need to know which types of product come from plants, which from animals, and which are produced by micro-organisms. For example:

Question 2

Which one of the following is obtained from a plant?

cheese • cotton • leather
polyester • silk • wool

1 _____

Living organisms and products

Millions of species of plants (flowering and non-flowering), animals (vertibrates and invertibrates) and micro-organisms live on earth. We grow some of them deliberately to provide food, clothing, furniture, medicines and other useful items. In most cases we use only part of the organism, though we may use different parts for different purposes.

	Type	Parts used	Types of product
Plants	trees	trunks and branches	wood (for furniture and as a fuel)
		sap	rubber
	food crops	vegetables	vegetables
		fruits and seeds	fruit, nuts and cereals
	other crops	various	cotton
			pharmaceuticals (medicines)
			dyes
Animals	farm animals	flesh	meat
		milk	dairy products (milk, butter and cheese)
		eggs	eggs
		skin (hide) or fleece	leather and wool
	fish	flesh	fish
	silkworms	silk fibres	woven silk fabric
Micro-organisms	yeasts	whole organism	bread and alcohol
	moulds (fungi)	whole organism	antibiotics (penicillin)
	bacteria	whole organism	cheese and yoghurt
			antibiotics

Classification

The **Linnaen system of classification** identifies and groups millions of different varieties of organisms. Organisms are given two names. A **genus** name which it shares with similar organisms and a unique **species** name.

Identification keys are like a set of clues helping scientists identify an organism.

Use the key below to identify these organisms:

(a) _____

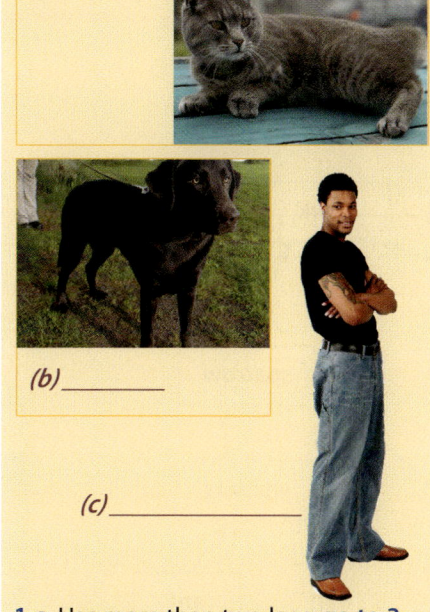

(b) _____

(c) _____

1 a Has more than two legs: **go to 3**
  b Has two legs or less: **go to 2**
2 a Has fur covering whole body: **go to 3**
  b Has no fur, but hair in places: *Homo sapiens* **(human beings)**
3 a Has pert, pointed ears: *Felis catus* **(cat)**
  b Has drooped ears without points: *Canis familiaris* **(dog)**

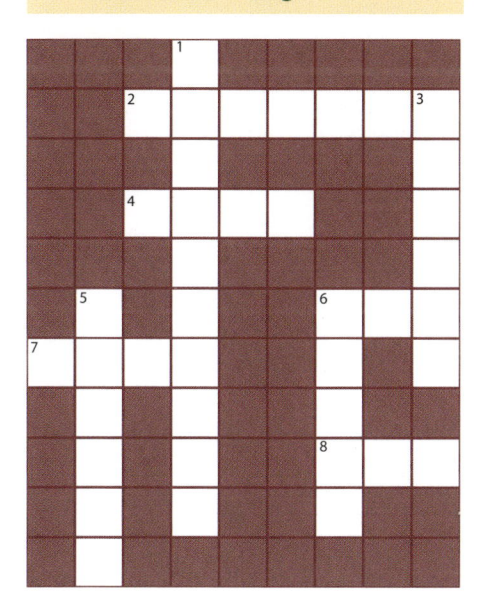

q&a

Q. *We get so many useful products from living things. Which ones do I need to know about?*

A. You should remember the ones listed in the table below. You'll probably know loads of others through your general knowledge.

Q. *What about plastics and other products made from oil or coal?*

A. Petroleum (crude oil) and coal were formed from dead creatures and plants. They aren't alive, so products made from them do not come from living organisms.

Q. *Is there a connection between organisms and organic chemicals?*

A. Yes. Organic chemicals were given this name because they were originally obtained from living (or dead) organisms. So, all the products we get from living things are made up of organic chemicals (carbon compounds).

Product	Where it comes from
cotton 	• seed heads of cotton plants. 
natural dyes 	• jeans are dyed with indigo, originally from the indigo plant • cochineal (a red dye) comes from tiny beetles! *However, most modern dyes are man-made.*
leather 	• animal skins (hides) - mainly from cows. 
pharmaceuticals 	• penicillin (an antibiotic) is produced by some types of mould • insulin for diabetics is obtained from pigs, and from genetically modified bacteria.
silk 	• silk worm cocoons. 
wool 	• sheep fleeces. 

Crossword clues ...

Across:
2. From animal skins (hides).
4. Spun by silkworms.
6. Colourful product from plants or animals.
7. From sheep fleeces.
8. This colour dye comes from tiny cochineal beetles.

Down:
1. Your doctor might prescribe tablets containing this if you have an infection. It's an antibiotic that comes from mould.
3. From the sap of a tree.
5. From the seed heads of cotton plants.
6. __ __ __ __ __ products (milk, butter and cheese) come from farm animals.

61

Biological systems

Ecosystems

An ecosystem is a community of different species which all depend upon each other to survive. Ecologists study ecosystems as large as oceans and as small as fields. They look at the energy flow within the ecosystem.

Interdependence of organisms

All organisms depend upon other organisms to survive.

For example:

Plants produce glucose and oxygen by photosynthesis. This is essential for the survival of organisms which can't photosynthesise.

Parasites, such as tape worm, live inside a host animal to survive.

Predators, such as panthers, depend upon there being enough prey to survive.

If the population of one type of organism in a food chain decreases (for example, because of disease or pollution) other organisms in the food chain will also be affected.

Food chains and webs

Food webs show the organisms present in an **ecosystem**. Arrows show the direction of energy flow between organisms. Arrows are drawn from one organism to another that eats it. So the producer is always the starting point. Food chains show a single line of energy transfer within a food web.

Question 1
How many food chains are there in this food web?

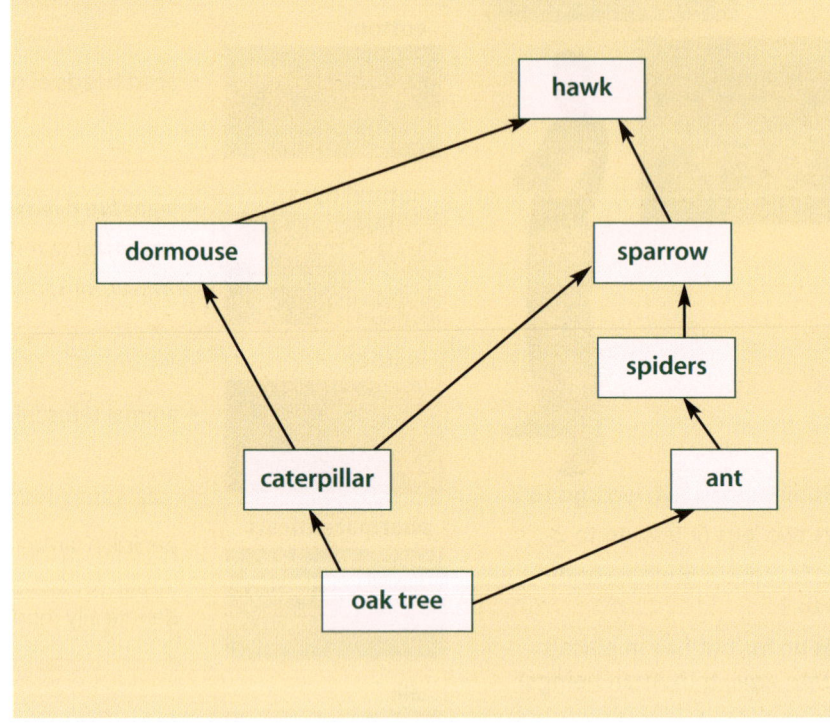

Terminology

Match the terms to the correct explanations. One of them's been done for you.

Producer	Eats only other animals.
Consumer	Eats only plants.
Omnivore	Produces its own food by photosynthesis.
Herbivore	Level in a food chain dependent on the method of feeding. All organisms in the same trophic level of a food web are the same number of energy transfers away from the producer of energy.
Carnivore	Bacteria or fungi. Feed on decaying matter.
Decomposer	Eats plants and animals.
Trophic level	Consumes other organisms for food.

62

Ecological pyramids

As energy is transferred from one trophic level to the next, energy is lost. Animals lose energy through respiration and digestive excretions. Energy flow between tropic levels of a food chain can be illustrated by three different types of ecological pyramids.

Pyramid of numbers	Pyramid of energy	Pyramid of biomasss
Shows the number of organisms at each level.	Shows the energy available per unit time at each level (normally kilocalories per metre squared per year)	Shows the biomass at each level (a representative sample of each level is dried and weighed)

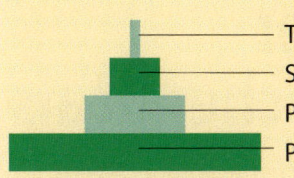

	Numbers	Energy	Biomass
Tertiary consumers	1	10 Kcal $^{-2}$ yr^{-1}	1 g m^{-2}
Secondary consumers	30	100 Kcal $^{-2}$ yr^{-1}	15 g m^{-2}
Primary consumers	100	1000 Kcal $^{-2}$ yr^{-1}	40 g m^{-2}
Producers	500	10000 Kcal $^{-2}$ yr^{-1}	800 g m^{-2}

Question 2
Give an advantage and disadvantage of each type of pyramid.

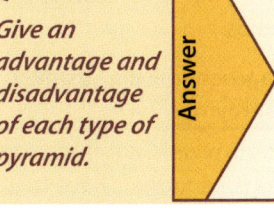

Answer

Pollution and the food chain

The build up of environmental pollution in food chains is a serious problem. The toxins that accumulate include heavy metals, organic pollutants and radiation. They come from products such as industrial chemicals, pesticides and some synthetic chemicals designed not to easily break down.

These pollutants accumulate in food chains because at each trophic level the toxic pollutants become more concentrated.

An example:
- Plankton in the sea absorb pollutants.
- Fish eat many contaminated plankton, so they end up with a higher concentration of toxins in their system than an individual plankton.
- Seals then eat many of these contaminated fish, increasing the concentration of the toxins again.
- Finally, polar bears eat the seals. The concentration of toxins is so high the bear's immune systems are damaged and they die.

Other types of pollution such as oil tanker spills in the ocean can greatly affect ecosystems. Even if only some organisms in a food chain are directly killed by the pollution this can have a knock on affect to all other organisms in the food web.

pollution

increasing concentration of toxins

Human activity and the environment

Greenhouse gases
Greenhouse gases allow sunlight to pass into the atmosphere but prevent heat escaping, trapping the sun's heat in the atmosphere. Greenhouse gases occur naturally but human activities such as burning fossil fuels are increasing their levels. This is causing the earth to warm up. Many species of organism are adapted to survive in particular climates. Climate change destroys habitats and this has a detrimental effect on many food chains.

Acid rain
Acid rain is caused by pollutant gases such as sulfur dioxide or nitrogen oxides reacting with oxygen in the air. This produces sulfuric acid and nitric acid in rain. Acid rain affects organisms sensitive to changes in the pH of soil or water.

Pollution indicator species
The presence or absence of some plants or animals can indicate whether a particular environment has been effected by pollution. For example some lichens don't grow if there are high levels of sulfur dioxide in the air.

Biological systems

Farming

A farm is an ecosystem. It's made of living and non-living things that interact and exchange energy. It's different from many ecosystems because much of the interaction is controlled by humans.

Feeding plants to feed the world

Plants need nutrients. Fertilisers replace the nutrients plants extract from the soil.

Artificial (man-made) fertilisers
- mainly **inorganic** compounds, such as ammonium sulfate and potassium nitrate.

Natural fertilisers (manure and compost)
- mainly **organic** - from living things;
- decay returns inorganic nutrients (N, P and K) to the soil.

Question 1: Write the names of N, P and K in the box ...

Answer:

Fertilisers increase crop yields. You get more food from the same area of land. Pasture land can feed more animals if fertiliser is spread on it (either artificial or the animals' own manure).

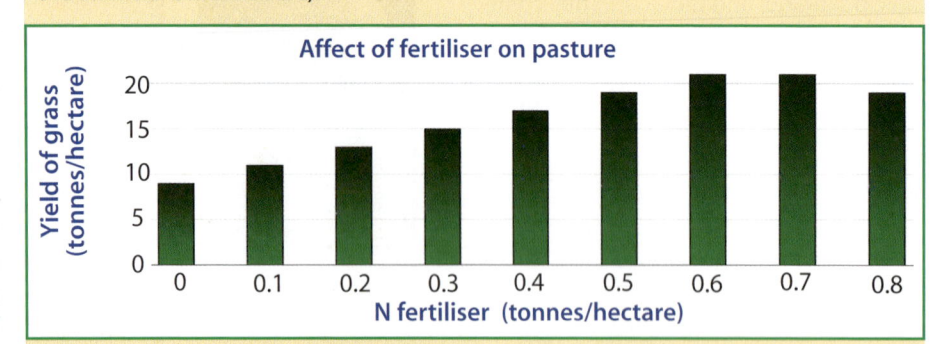

Affect of fertiliser on pasture

N fertiliser (tonnes/hectare)	Yield of grass (tonnes/hectare)
0	~9
0.1	~11
0.2	~13
0.3	~15
0.4	~17
0.5	~19
0.6	~21
0.7	~21
0.8	~19

Question 2
(a) Why is it pointless to apply too much fertiliser to a crop? (Look at the chart.)
(b) Explain why too much fertiliser could actually be harmful.

Answer:

Fertilisers, both artificial and natural, can cause problems if they are washed into water supplies. The Environment Agency monitors the quality of our rivers to detect possible problems and recommend suitable action.

Other agrochemicals

Crops grow better without weeds, pests and diseases. These can be controlled using agrochemicals or natural methods.

Man-made agrochemicals - usually applied by spraying:

- Herbicides kill weeds. But they may also kill crops, so farmers have to …
  - apply them before crops are grown;
  - use a selective weedkiller that kills weeds but not the crop.
- Pesticides kill plant pests that eat part of the plant (mainly insects and their larvae, such as caterpillars). But they may also kill useful insects such as bees and ladybirds.
- Fungicides kill moulds and fungi that cause diseases in crops.

Natural methods avoid using synthetic chemicals:

- Mechanical weeding (hoeing / digging / mulching).
- Biological pest control - introducing natural predators to kill insect pests, such as lacewing larvae or parasitic wasps that kill greenfly larvae.
- Natural insecticides. You get these from flowers, such as pyrethrum.

Biosphere two

There are other, more extreme, examples of controlled eco-systems.

The **Biosphere 2 Project**, for example, was set up to see if people could live and work in a closed biosphere. People were sealed inside a giant glass structure in Arizona for two years - along with hundreds of plants and animals.

They had to make sure their resources were constantly recycled so all the plants, animals and people had everything they needed to live.

It's hoped that this sort of biosphere could one day be used in space, so that humans can colonise distant planets.

Inside Biosphere 2: pictured are the Savanna (*foreground*) and Ocean (*background*) sections.

64

Comparing intensive and organic farming methods

Farms may produce crops, animals, or both. **Intensive** and **organic** methods are very different.
- **Intensive** means squeezing a lot into a small space or time, trying to produce the maximum amount of crops or animals.
- **Organic** means using only natural biological materials and processes - no artificial agrochemicals.

Intensive farmers ...	Organic farmers ...
use synthetic inorganic fertilisers to increase crop yields (including grass for animals);	use manure and/or compost (animals manure their own pastures);
concentrate on certain crops or animals;	use crop rotation (including peas / beans / clover that fix nitrogen);
use synthetic herbicides and pesticides (to eliminate crops' competitors);	use mechanical weeding and natural pest control;
remove hedgerows to make larger fields (easier to work with machines);	retain hedges (helps wildlife);
keep animals caged or penned to restrict their movement and provide warmth, for example, battery hens (larger animals graze fields in summer);	allow animals to roam free in fields (with shelter from bad weather);
control the diet and feeding of indoor animals to increase their weight gain;	may supply some food, but animals free to graze and forage for natural foods;
use growth hormones, so animals grow and mature faster.	provide conditions for animals to grow well naturally.

Question 3
On a mixed farm, crop rotation includes years when a field is used for grazing animals instead of growing a crop. How does this help?

Answer

q&a

Q. Why are animals on intensive farms kept in cages or pens to restrict their movement?

A. The animals use less energy, so need less food for the same amount of growth. Less food energy is used for movement, so more used for gain in weight, or egg production.

Q. What's special about peas, beans and clover?

A. These plants have nodules (small lumps) on their roots, containing bacteria, which 'fix' nitrogen from the air. They convert nitrogen into ammonia and other compounds that plants need. After harvest, the roots continue 'fixation', adding nutrients to the soil without using fertiliser.

Intensive Farming

Advantages	Disadvantages
More machinery (less labour needed).	Machinery burns fossil fuels.
Using agrochemicals gives higher yields (more crops or animals from less farmland).	Making agrochemicals uses up finite mineral and energy resources.
More economic (produces large amounts of food at cheaper prices).	
	Environmental problems: - eutrophication of waterways - pesticides can kill useful insects - pesticide residues in food chain
	Animals kept in unnatural conditions

Organic Farming

Advantages	Disadvantages
Less use of expensive machinery and fuel.	More jobs by hand - more labour needed.
Less use of finite resources - plant and animal waste recycled as compost and manure.	Lower yields - increases cost per item or per tonne.
	Higher production costs.
No environmental problems from mechanical weeding or biological pest control.	Less effective control of weeds and pests.
Animals live more natural lives.	

Biological systems

How organisms grow

When organisms develop and grow they increase in size and mass. They do this by cell division and cell enlargement. To be able to grow, organisms need food. Plants and some bacteria make their own food by photosynthesis. Animals have to obtain food by eating plants or other organisms. Plants and animals turn their food into glucose which they can turn into energy during respiration.

Sunlight: Energy for life

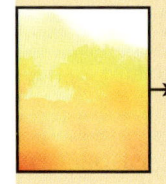

Energy is needed to put together the chemicals a plant or animal needs to live and grow. Animals get their energy from food. Some eat plants (for example, rabbits eat dandelions). Some eat other animals that have eaten plants (for example, wolves eat rabbits). Plants make their own food by photosynthesis, using energy from sunlight. No sunlight, no plants, no life.

What is photosynthesis?

Synthesis = putting small parts together to build up something more complex.

Photo = using light (as in photography).

Photosynthesis does what it says. It uses light energy to build larger molecules (glucose) from small ones (carbon dioxide and water). However, it's not that simple. A solution of carbon dioxide (fizzy mineral water) tastes sour, not sweet. It contains carbonic acid, H_2CO_3, not glucose, $C_6H_{12}O_6$.

$$CO_2 + H_2O \rightarrow H_2CO_3$$

In photosynthesis, six molecules of each react, gradually building up a glucose molecule in several stages powered by sunlight.

$$6CO_2 + 6H_2O \rightarrow C_6H_{12}O_6 + ?$$

Question 1
What is the other product of this reaction? In other words, what does '?' stand for in the equation?

Answer:

How photosynthesis works

Green plants can photosynthesise. It takes place in the chloroplasts (see *Cells and their contents* page 70-71). Chloroplasts are green because they contain chlorophyll, a green pigment. Chlorophyll is needed for making glucose. Chlorophyll keeps the production of glucose going, as long as it's light and there's a supply of carbon dioxide and water.

Carbon dioxide moves into leaves through the stomata by diffusion. Water is absorbed into root hairs by osmosis. It passes up the stem to the leaves (see *Cells and their contents*, page 70-71). Carbon dioxide and water react, with the help of chlorophyll, inside the chloroplasts. The overall reaction is:

$$6CO_2 + 6H_2O + \text{energy} \rightarrow C_6H_{12}O_6 + 6O_2$$

carbon dioxide + water + energy → glucose + oxygen

Chlorophyll is green because green light is reflected when sunlight shines on it. The other colours of the spectrum are absorbed. The energy from this absorbed light provides the energy for the photosynthesis reactions.

Question 2
(a) Which word describes the role of chlorophyll in this reaction: reactant, product, catalyst, solute or solvent?
(b) Is photosynthesis an exothermic or endothermic reaction? How can you tell?

Answer:

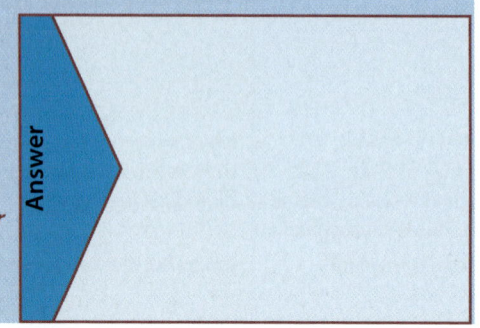

Photosynthesis: the comings and goings

Question 3
Label the diagram using these words:
- water
- sunlight
- glucose
- oxygen
- carbon dioxide

66

Controlling growth

During human development cell division takes place throughout the whole body. The child gradually increases in size until it becomes an adult. Cell division and growth stop. However, some cells continue to grow and be replaced throughout the lifetime of the organism. Growth is controlled by hormones.

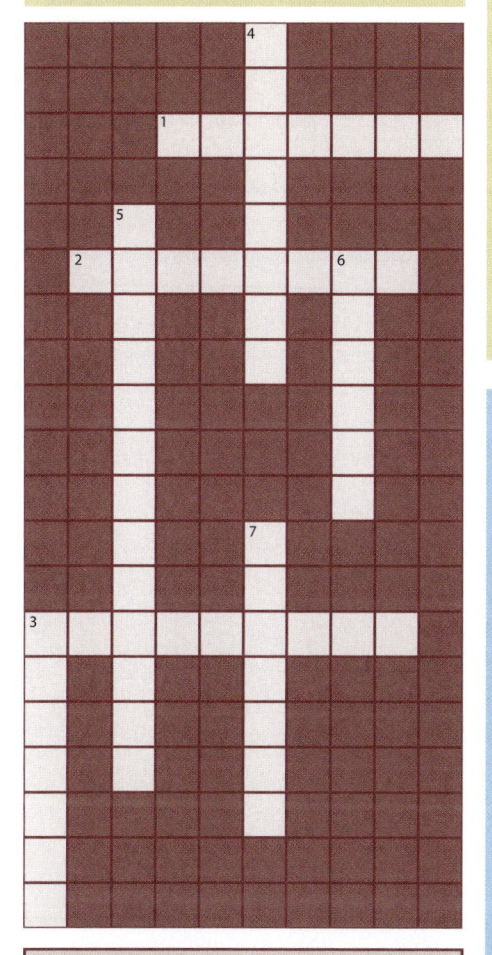

Crossword clues ...

Across:
1. cell division which replicates body cells
2. internal factor limiting growth when hormones and external environment do not
3. gland at the base of the brain which secretes growth hormones

Down:
3. stage of growth when animal becomes sexually mature
4. mineral plants need to make protein
5. triggers embryo to develop
6. disease caused by uncontrolled cell growth
7. cell division which creates sex cells

Making best use of photosynthesis

The World's population is increasing. To grow enough food for everybody, scientists and farmers use their knowledge of photosynthesis. How well plants grow depends on: temperature, light, carbon dioxide and water.

Horticulturists grow crops in glasshouses. They can control these four conditions artificially to give the best rate of photosynthesis.

Question 4
How would the following affect a crop grown in a glasshouse?
(a) Using electric heaters to increase the temperature during cooler weather.
(b) Burning gas or oil instead of using electric heaters.
(c) Using electric lighting to extend the hours of 'daylight'.

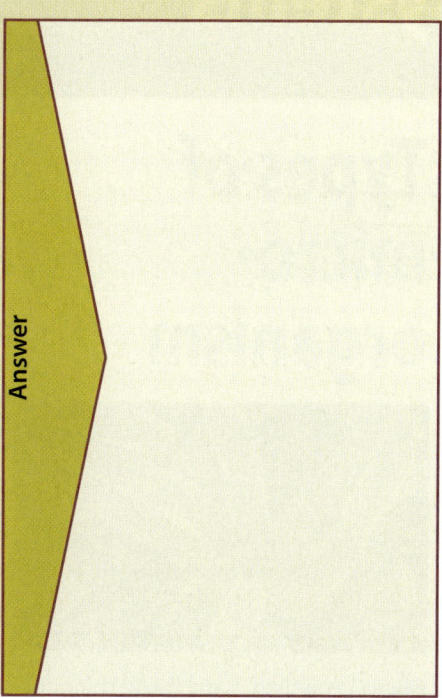

Plant nutrients

To grow properly, and stay healthy, plants also need other nutrients. They absorb these from solutions of minerals in the soil, by diffusion into root hair cells.

The main plant nutrients are:

- **nitrogen (N):** as nitrate ions (NO_3^-) - to make proteins that all cells need to grow, especially stems and leaves
- **phosphorus (P):** as phosphate ions (PO_4^{3-}) - for strong roots
- **potassium (K):** as potassium ions (K^+) - for good flowers and fruit.

All plants need all three minerals. But they may need different proportions, depending on whether they are leaf crops (for example, cabbage), root crops (for example, carrots) or fruit crops (for example, strawberries).

Plants also need magnesium ions (Mg^{2+}) and small amounts of other metal ions such as calcium and iron. Magnesium is essential because plants need it for making chlorophyll.

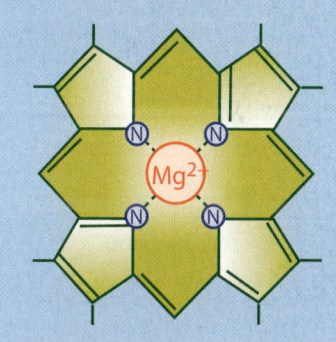

Chlorophyll has a magnesium ion at its centre

Respiration: releasing the captured energy

Glucose made by photosynthesis is the plant's food. It goes to all the plant's cells to provide them with energy. Energy is released from glucose by respiration, which takes place in the mitochondria. Glucose reacts with oxygen in a complex series of reactions. The end result is:

$$C_6H_{12}O_6 + 6O_2 \rightarrow 6CO_2 + 6H_2O + \text{energy}$$

glucose + oxygen → carbon dioxide + water + energy

This reverses the effect of photosynthesis. Energy absorbed from sunlight is released again in every cell. Plants convert spare glucose into starch by joining glucose molecules into long chains. Starch is a polymer of glucose. It stores the energy for later

67

Biological systems

Micro-organisms

Types of micro-organism

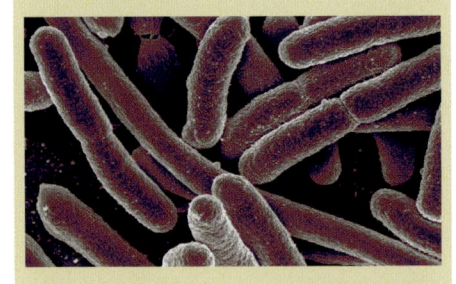

Micro-organism = any living thing too small to see without a **micro**scope.

Large groups (colonies) of bacteria, yeasts or moulds can be seen.

Fungi (singular = fungus)
- Largest micro-organisms.
- Some multi-celled - form visible groups of thread-like structures.
- Others single-celled, such as:
  - yeasts;
  - moulds.

Note: Not all fungi are micro-organisms; some, such as mushrooms, are larger.

Bacteria (singular = bacterium)
- Single-celled - cells have no nucleus, but still have DNA.
- Spherical or rod-shaped.

Unscramble these jumbled words using the clues to help you ...

(a) NIASITCOTBI

Medicines that have been made from natural substances produced by micro-organisms:

_____

(b) BITCARAE

Micro-organisms that multiply every 20 minutes:

_____

Useful micro-organisms

As micro-organisms live and multiply they produce a wide variety of by-products. Many of these are used as foods or medicines. Examples:

Micro-organism	Food product	Medicine
fungus	mycoprotein	
yeasts	bread, beer and wine	
moulds	blue cheese	penicillin (an antibiotic)
bacteria	yoghurt, cheese	insulin, antibiotics

Fermentation

Fermentation means growing certain micro-organisms in a closed container with no air. *Note: 'growing' = reproduction, not increasing size.* The micro-organisms obtain energy by **anaerobic respiration**. They break down substances (such as sugars) without using oxygen. Temperature is controlled (usually 30-40 °C) for maximum rate of reproduction. Several useful products are made this way.

Bread, beer and wine - by alcoholic fermentation

- Yeasts ferment glucose into alcohol (ethanol) and carbon dioxide gas.

  $C_6H_{12}O_6 \rightarrow 2C_2H_5OH + 2CO_2$
  glucose $\rightarrow$ ethanol + carbon dioxide

- In bread-making, carbon dioxide bubbles make the dough rise.
- For beer, the sugar (maltose) comes from germinating barley. Soaking in water dissolves the sugar. This dilute solution is fermented to give 3-5% alcohol.
- For wine, the sugar (fructose) is in the grapes. No water is added. Grape juice is fermented to give 10-15% alcohol.
- The carbon dioxide provides the 'fizz' in beer and sparkling wines.

Yoghurt - by lactic acid fermentation

- *Lactobacilli*, a type of bacteria, ferment lactose (the sugar in milk) into lactic acid.
- The acid coagulates the casein (a protein) in milk. The milk thickens. This is yoghurt.

Antibiotics

Antibiotics, such as penicillin, are chemical compounds produced by certain bacteria and fungi. They kill other bacteria (but **not** viruses).

- *Penicillium* mould (a fungus) ferments a mixture of glucose and ammonia.
- As it grows, it produces penicillin as a by-product.
- The penicillin is extracted and purified.

Question 1

In processes that use micro-organisms, they are kept warm, but not too hot. What happens if the temperature is:

(a) too low? (b) too high?

Answer

Making protein

Quorn mycoprotein, a vegetarian alternative to meat, is produced by a fungus.
- *Fusarium* fungus is fed with glucose and nutrients.
- Oxygen is added.
- Harvested fungus, rich in protein, is coloured, flavoured and textured to imitate meat.

Complete this paragraph, selecting the correct words from the list below ...

LACTIC ACID • BACTERIA • ACIDITY • MILK • LACTOSE • COAGULATE • CASEIN

To make yoghurt, a 'lactic acid' bacteria starter culture is added to _____. In warm conditions the _____ feed off the main sugar present in milk, _____, and produce _____. This increases the _____ of the mixture. This makes the main milk protein, _____, thicken and set together (in other words _____) and form yoghurt.

Food preparation

Places where food is prepared (domestic or industrial kitchens) are potential hot spots for the spread of harmful micro-organisms.

Things we use in the kitchen such as cloths, chopping boards, knives and other utensils are places where micro-organisms such as bacteria may thrive.

So, what can we do about it?

Wash

Did you know some bacteria can stay alive on your hands for three hours? And a thousand times more bacteria spread from damp hands than dry hands. So:
- wash and dry your hands thoroughly when handling food - before, between and after;
- use warm water and a detergent
- rinse with clean water
- dry with a dry towel, paper towel or air dryer.

Sterilise

Kill bacteria on equipment by sterilisation. This can be done by:
- heating them above the temperature at which the bacteria can survive (moist heat is better than dry heat)
- heating them in an autoclave, using steam under pressure at temperatures of around 120 °C
- washing them in a disinfectant such as bleach.

Disinfect

Kill or prevent the growth of bacteria with disinfectants (also known as antiseptics).

Some products are labelled **disinfectant** and others **antiseptic**. Bleach is an example of a disinfectant that kills bacteria. You will find many antiseptics in supermarkets. For example, *Dettol, Germolene* and *Savlon*.

Question 2
(a) List some things that you would sterilise using disinfectants rather than high temperatures.
(b) Why is it important to dry your hands thoroughly after washing them?

Answer

Biological systems

Cells and their contents

Cells are the building blocks of all organisms. Some micro-organisms such as bacteria consist of a single cell. More complex organisms consist of multiple cells, and in some organisms some cells are specialised for different functions.

What are cells?

Prison cells hold prisoners. Electric cells hold chemicals for making electricity. Usually, cells are joined together to make something larger - a prison, or a battery. Bees' honeycomb is made of cells, which they fill with honey.

Plants and animals are also made up of cells joined together. But these cells are tiny. They are made up of chemicals. These include simple compounds like sodium chloride, large molecules like haemoglobin, and complex molecules such as deoxyribonucleic acid (DNA).

Each cell contains different parts, called organelles. All organisms are made of one or more cells.

Question 1
Which type of cells contain haemoglobin?

Answer

Cells: The Guided Tour

What's in a cell?

Using a light microscope we can see the parts of a cell. Each part has a purpose. Some are found in both plant and animal cells. Others are found only in plant cells.

Question 2
Complete the plural: one mitochondrion, two or more mitochond____.

Answer

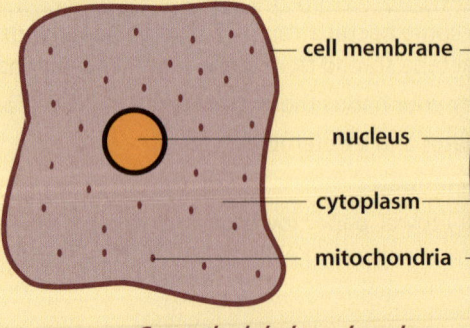

Animal Cell
- cell membrane
- nucleus
- cytoplasm
- mitochondria

Cover the labels and see how many you can remember.

Plant Cell
- cell wall
- vacuole
- chloroplast

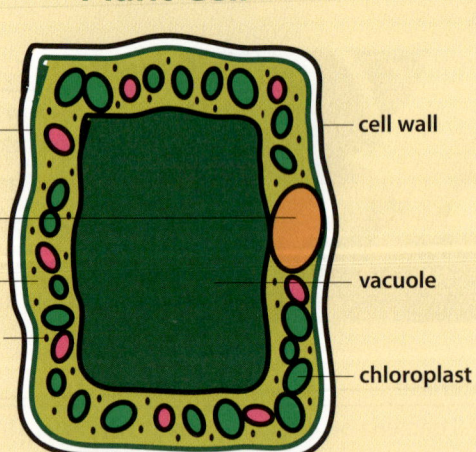

What does each part do?

Cell membrane: a thin *bag* that holds the cell's parts. Chemicals pass through this membrane to get in and out of the cell.

Cytoplasm: a jelly-like solution of chemicals where the cell stores its food.

Mitochondrion: where cell respiration takes place to release energy for the organism to use.

Nucleus: contains DNA, which carries the organism's genetic code.

Plant cells also have ...

Cell wall: made of cellulose. It makes a plant cell more rigid.

Chloroplast: where photosynthesis takes place to make food for the plant. It contains chlorophyll.

Vacuole: a *bag* of cell sap (a solution of sugar and various salts). It helps keep the cell rigid when it is full.

Question 3
Why don't animal cells contain chloroplasts?

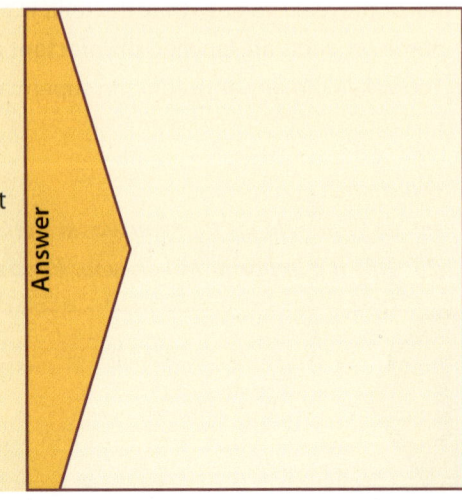

Answer

Proteins

Cells contain many different types of protein from muscle fibres to enzymes. The structure of a protein is essential for its function. Proteins are made up of a 'string' of amino acids in a particular order.

Proteins are fibrous, e.g. muscle and hair, or globuler, e.g. enzymes.

The enzyme has a unique structure which allows it to bind to other specific chemicals.

Ribbon diagram of the 3D-structure of a globular protein

Scientists use diagrams like this to help them analyse the structure of different proteins to discover more about how each works.

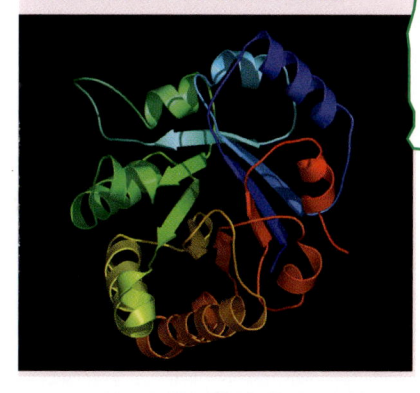

Find the seven cell parts. Highlight the three that are only found in plant cells.

```
M C M X C N
T I H E R E I M
C T L M X L L H
Y Y O O B V L N V D
G T C R R U W S A E
A O H O A F A U C F
C P O P N C L E U F
C L N L E V L L O Z
T A D A Z I U C L S
S S R S T B K U E R
M I T Z S D N Y
D O E D P H M T
N F S G H P
```

Chemical compounds in cells

- Every living organism is made up of a collection of cells.
- Every cell is made up of chemical compounds.
- So, every living organism is made up of chemical compounds.

Nearly all of these compounds are made from: **C, H, O, N** and smaller amounts of: **Ca, P, K, Cl, S, Na, Mg, Fe**. These are the symbols for the elements.

Write the names of the elements in the picture.

The main types of compounds in cells are:

- **carbohydrates** - such as sugars, starch and glycogen, to provide energy;
- **fats and oils** - used to store spare energy from food;
- **proteins** - compounds that form muscle, hair, wool and so on, and also enzymes for chemical reactions in cells.

Question 4
Which chemical elements make up:
(a) carbohydrates (b) proteins?

> Answer

Diffusion and osmosis: the comings and goings in cells

Cells are tiny chemical factories. They take in chemicals, and change them into the different chemicals the organism needs. They 'export' these to cells that need them. Chemicals move in and out of cells by diffusion through the cell membrane.

Diffusion

Liquids and gases consist of particles constantly moving around. These particles can pass through cell membranes in both directions. We say they **diffuse** through the membrane.

The particles move from where there are a lot of them (high concentration) to where there are less (low concentration). But the particles (molecules and ions) must be very small, for example: oxygen and carbon dioxide molecules, sodium and chloride ions.

Diffusion and respiration

Respiration takes place in cells. It's how you get energy from food. During respiration **oxygen in cells is used up**. Its concentration decreases. Because its concentration is higher outside, oxygen molecules diffuse into the cell.

During respiration **carbon dioxide is made** in the cell. Because its concentration is higher in the cell than outside the cell, carbon dioxide molecules diffuse out of the cell.

Question 5
In which direction do carbon dioxide and oxygen pass through a cell membrane, during: (a) photosynthesis (b) respiration?

> Answer

Osmosis

Water molecules move into and out of cells through the cell membrane. This is called **osmosis**. Water passes from where there are a lot of water molecules (a dilute solution) to where there are less water molecules (a concentrated solution).

Note: A concentrated solution contains more dissolved solute and less water, so the concentration of water is low.

Osmosis in your kidneys removes excess water from your blood. Osmosis of water into plant cells keeps the vacuoles full and the cells more rigid. Without this, the cells go limp and the plant wilts.

Biological systems

How cells divide

There are two types of cell division. One type called mitosis replicates cells during growth and repair. The second called meiosis produces gamete (sperm / egg) cells with half the number of chromosomes as body cells.

The need for new cells

Living things need new cells for three reasons:
growth - the organism increases its size
repair - parts die and are replaced, for example, skin cells
reproduction - to produce more organisms.
To produce extra cells, a process of cell division is needed.

The results of cell division

There are two types of cell division:

mitosis - the cell produces **two identical** copies of itself.

- Mitosis occurs in all types of organism.
- The new cells are used for growth and repair.
- Some organisms, such as strawberry plants and ferns, also **reproduce** by mitosis. Offspring are identical to the parent. They are clones. This is an example of **asexual** reproduction.

meiosis - the cell divides twice, producing **four different cells**, called gametes.

- Meiosis occurs only when an organism produces gametes (eggs and sperm).
- Gametes are sex cells that contain half the genetic information of a parent.
- One gamete from each parent combine to produce a new organism.
- Offspring are different from their parents.

Question 1
Name the male and female gametes in (a) plants (b) animals

Answer

q & a

Q. I get confused between mitosis and meiosis. How can I remember which is which?

A. Try a memory aid in which the first letters remind you, such as:

Mitosis - **M**akes **i**dentical **t**ypes of cell - for growth, replacement and identical offspring.

Meiosis - **M**akes **e**xclusive **i**ndividuals - offspring with their own sets of characteristics.

Q. Why do cells divide differently for asexual and sexual reproduction?

A. It's all to do with getting the right genes.

Asexual reproduction makes a new organism just like the original. It must have the same collection of genes. Mitosis makes identical copies of all the chromosomes (which carry the genes). A complete set is passed on.

Sexual reproduction is designed to produce genetic diversity. Meiosis passes on half the chromosomes from each parent, so the new individual has a different mix of genes.

What are genes?

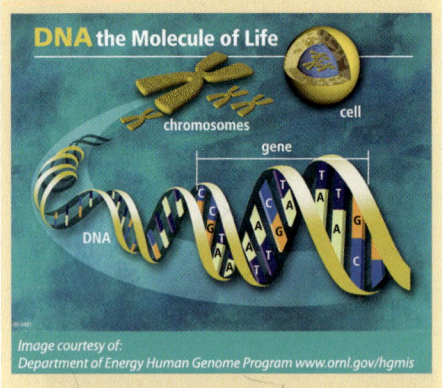

Image courtesy of:
Department of Energy Human Genome Program www.ornl.gov/hgmis

Cells develop into complete organisms. The **genetic code** is the instructions they follow.

- The code is carried by **DNA** in the **chromosomes** found in the nucleus of every cell.
- A **gene** is a section of a chromosome containing the DNA code that controls one characteristic.
- The 46 human chromosomes (23 pairs) contain more than 30,000 genes.
- The code is made up of **nucleotides**. They contain a **phosphate**, **deoxynbose sugar** and one of four **bases**:
  - adenine (A)
  - cytosine (C)
  - thymione (T)
  - guanine (G)

The order of these bases determines the protein that is made when the code is interpreted.

- Different proteins have different functions depending on their structure.

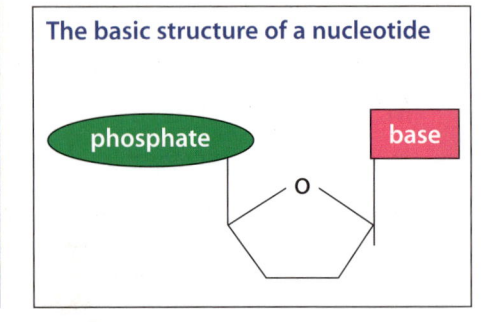

The basic structure of a nucleotide

phosphate — base

How cell division works

Imagine a journey into a cell to watch it dividing. The sequences below show what you would see:

Mitosis
- for growth and repair.

Meiosis
- for the production of gametes (eggs and sperm).

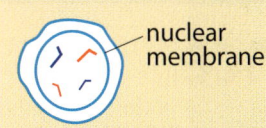

Original cell
Each cell contains a nucleus. Chromosomes are found inside it. These are made up of DNA which carries a sequence of genes. *Note: only four chromosomes are shown here for simplicity (two large, two small).*

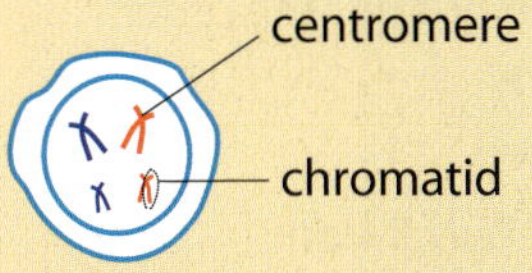

Replication
The chromosomes copy themselves, so the nucleus contains two complete sets. The copies, called **chromatids**, are joined to the original at the **centromere**.

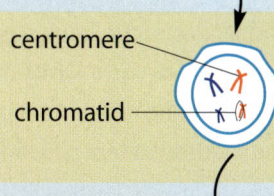

Mitosis stages

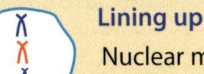

Lining up
Nuclear membrane disappears. Centromeres line up across the centre of the cell.

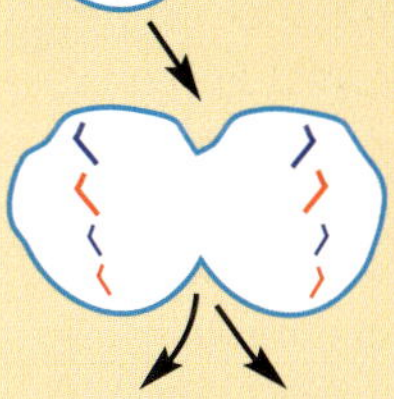

Separation
Centromeres are pulled to opposite sides of the cell, separating the two sets of chromosomes.

Division
The cell divides in two, and membranes re-form around each nucleus. The result is two daughter cells identical to the original.

Question 2
Sometimes a mistake occurs during replication, so that the copied cell is not quite identical. What is this called?

Answer:

Meiosis stages

Pairing
Nuclear membrane disappears. Chromosomes from each parent pair up in the centre of the cell.

Crossing over
Pairs swap some of their genes. These new chromosomes are no longer identical.

Separation
Chromosomes separate and are pulled to opposite sides of the cell.

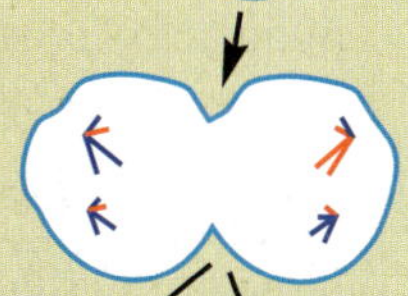

Division
The cell divides in two, and membranes re-form around each nucleus. This gives two cells, each with half the original number of chromosomes.

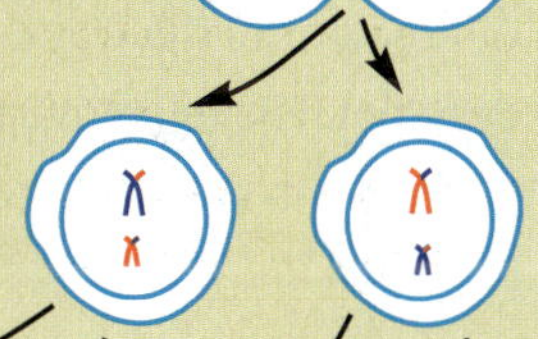

Further division
Each of the two cells divides into two again, following the lining up, separation and division stages of mitosis. This results in four non-identical gametes.

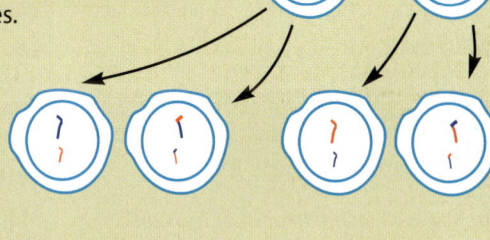

Fertilisation

When a male and female gamete meet during fertilisation, they join together to form a new cell, which contains the full number of chromosomes. Human cells contain 23 pairs of chromosomes. The gametes (sperm cells and eggs) each contain 23 single chromosomes. So the fertilised egg contains 46 chromosomes (23 pairs).

Question 3
Explain why ... (a) children inherit some characteristics from each parent (b) children of the same parents don't inherit the same characteristics.

Answer:

Biological systems

Passing on genes

We get characteristics from our parents by **genetic inheritance**.
One mechanism of inheritance is called **monhybrid inheritance**.

Characteristics are inherited

Organisms of the same species reproduce to form fertile offspring. Their genetic make-up depends on the method of reproduction.

Asexual reproduction (by mitosis)

- All offspring genetically identical to the parent. They inherit all characteristics.

Sexual reproduction (by meiosis)

- Offspring genetically similar, but all slightly different. They inherit general features of their species, and a mixture of **individual** characteristics from each parent.

Genes control the way every cell develops. They determine what type of organism the cells become, and also each individual's differences.

Question 1

(a) What is the name given to egg cells and sperm cells? What is special about these cells?

(b) Suggest two features of humans that every child inherits.

(c) Suggest two individual characteristics of its parents that a child inherits.

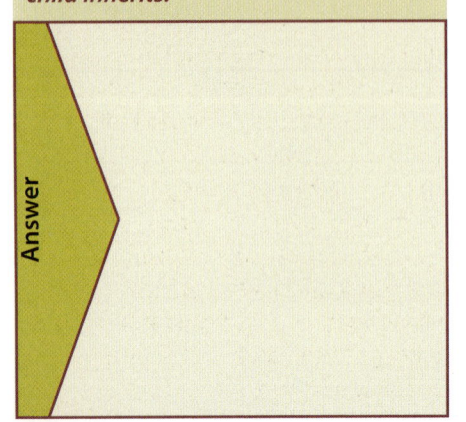

Answer

Monohybrid inheritance

Chromosomes come in pairs - one from each parent. They may contain different versions of the same gene. For example, the offspring may inherit a gene for blue eye colour from one parent and a gene for brown eye colour from the other parent. Different forms of the same gene are called **alleles**.

- One allele is **dominant**. Its instructions are always followed.
- The other allele is **recessive**. Its instructions are followed only if **both** chromosomes contain the recessive allele.
- Cells contain chromosomes with one allele from each parent. These pairs give rise to the **genotype**.

   Individuals with a pair of the same allele are **homozygous** for that characteristic.
   - **Homozygous dominant** means two dominant alleles.
   - **Homozygous recessive** means two recessive alleles.

   Those with one dominant and one recessive allele are **heterozygous**.
- The characteristics themselves (such as brown or blue eyes) are called **phenotypes**.
- We represent alleles by single letters - capital for dominant, lower case for recessive.

Example

The brown eyes allele (**B**) is dominant. The one for blue eyes (**b**) is recessive. There are four possible genotypes (pairs of alleles).

- **BB** (homozygous dominant), **Bb** and **bB** (both heterozygous) all give brown eyes, because of the dominant allele.
- Only **bb** (homozygous recessive) gives blue eyes.

Question 2

Decide whether the following are dominant or recessive, homozygous or heterozygous. The first one's been done for you:

Genotype	dominant or recessive?	homozygous or heterozygous?
H H	dominant	homozygous
H h		
h H		
hh		

Egg cells contain half the genes from one parent. Sperm cells contain half the genes from the other parent. So, fertilisation produces a new cell containing one allele of each gene from each parent.

We don't know which egg cells and sperm cells will join, so can't predict which alleles the new cell will inherit.

However, we can work out the chances of the offspring developing a particular characteristic (**phenotype**). **To do this …**

Step 1. Draw a table with the genotype (two alleles) of one parent on the left and the other across the top - it doesn't matter which is which.

Step 2. Into each box, copy the alleles from the left and from above. (This gives four combinations - each of one parent's alleles combined with each of the other's.)

Step 3. Decide what genotypes and phenotypes the four offspring have.

Monohybrid inheritance (continued ...)

Example one ...

Both parents have brown eyes - same **phenotype**.
Both parent's alleles are **Bb** - same **genotype** (**heterozygous**).

Step 1

	Father's genotype	
Mother's genotype	B	b
B		
b		

Step 2

	Father's genotype	
Mother's genotype	B	b
B	BB	Bb
b	bB	bb

Step 3

	Father's genotype	
Mother's genotype	B	b
B	BB	Bb
b	bB	bb

Four possible genotypes of offspring.

genotypes: BB, Bb and Bb
phenotype: All brown eyes

genotype: bb
phenotype: blue eyes

So, chance of blue eyes = 1 in 4.

complete this example ...

Mother has brown eyes; father has blue eyes - different phenotypes.
Mother's genotype is **Bb**; father's genotype is **bb** - different genotypes (mother is **heterozygous**; father is **homozygous recessive**).

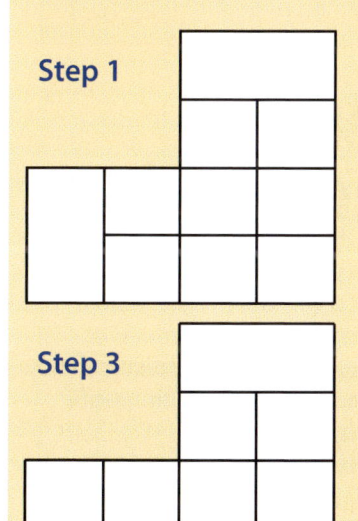

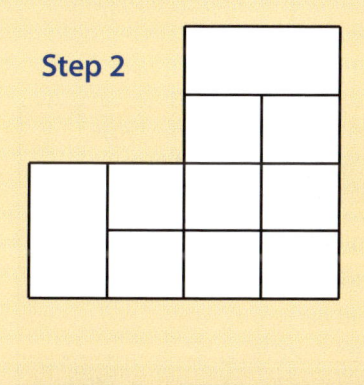

Step 1

Step 2

Step 3

Question 3
A man has genotype BB, so has brown eyes. His partner has blue eyes. What is the chance of their baby having blue eyes? You may need to use a separate piece of paper to sketch the three steps.

Answer

Inherited conditions and diseases

Some diseases are inherited. For example:

Sickle cell syndrome
Abnormal haemoglobin in red blood cells. Blood cells become sickle shaped, less flexible and more fragile. They don't travel through blood vessels easily and can cause clots to form preventing blood flow. Sickle cells die sooner than normal cells, so the person is often **anaemic**, (lack enough red blood cells, and therefore oxygen).

Multiple sclerosis
A neurological autoimmune disorder. The protective myelin sheaths that surround nerve fibres become damaged. This affects the central nervous system. Symptoms include bladder and bowel dysfunction, emotional changes, memory problems, inability to walk properly and many others.

Parkinson's disease
Normally occurs in older people. A degenerative neurological disease. The cells of a part of the brain which produce a chemical called dopamine begin to die. Symptoms include trembling arms and legs, slower voluntary movements and rigid muscles. Some people also develop senile dementia.

Cystic fibrosis
Occurs when the faulty gene is inherited from both parents. Specialised glands which produce digestive enzymes and the mucus which lines the respiratory tract produce overly thick and sticky secretions. Eventually the glands become blocked and form cysts. Symptoms include poor growth (from ineffective digestion), lung damage (from repeated coughing and infection), pancreatic damage sometimes causing diabetes and liver damage (small ducts in the liver become blocked).

Biological systems

Controlling gene inheritance

There are two main ways humans can control genetic inheritance, **selective breeding** or **genetic engineering**. Selective breeding involves repeated selection and crossing of organisms with a favoured characteristic over many generations. Genetic engineering is a more direct method, transferring individual genes directly into foreign cells to develop organisms with desired characteristics.

What is selective breeding?

Selective breeding aims to improve the characteristics of a species.

Individuals showing the required characteristics or traits are chosen for breeding. Bigger yields of crops, flowers with a strong scent, and leaner meat are examples of characteristics that have been selected.

For example, to produce leaner pigs, breeders …

1. select pigs with the least fat and mate them. Some offspring will be lean, but some may also inherit **undesirable** characteristics;
2. select the best of the lean offspring, and mate these;
3. continue selecting and breeding over many generations. The proportion of lean pigs gradually increases.

But this isn't new. Domestic and farm animals and plants were bred from wild species thousands of years ago. Selective breeding has been improving them ever since.

Question 1
A garden centre sells seeds for 'Mammoth Onions', which grow much larger than normal.

Suggest how the 'Mammoth' variety was developed from normal onions.

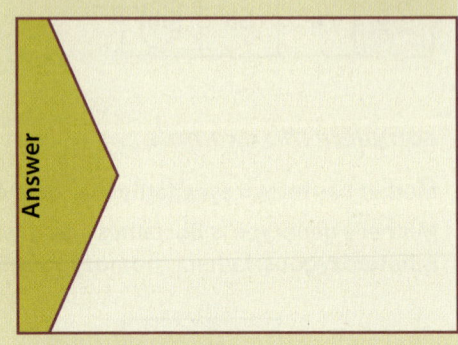

Answer:

q&a

Q. *Is selective breeding the same as cross-breeding?*

A. Cross-breeding is selective breeding using parents from two different (but related) **breeds** of animal or **varieties** of plant. It is used to develop animals and plants with the best characteristics of both parents. For example:

- strawberries that give large fruits with a good flavour
- new varieties of roses, with attractive flowers and strong scent
- sheep that produce high quality meat *and* wool
- beef cattle suitable for hot countries

For plants, the two varieties are cross-pollinated by dusting pollen from one onto the stigmas in flowers of the other.

For animals, good examples of each breed are mated to produce cross-bred young.

Only organisms of the same type (genus) can be cross-bred. For example:

- two breeds of dog ✓
- two varieties of rose ✓
- dog and cat ✗
- rose and sunflower ✗

Offspring cross-bred from two different species are often infertile. They cannot breed further. For example:

- mule (horse + donkey)
- ortanique (orange + tangerine)

Question 2
Which of the following cross-breeds cannot exist, and why not?

(a) liger (lion + tiger)
(b) mermaid (fish + woman)
(c) tayberry (blackberry + raspberry)
(d) carron (carrot + lemon)

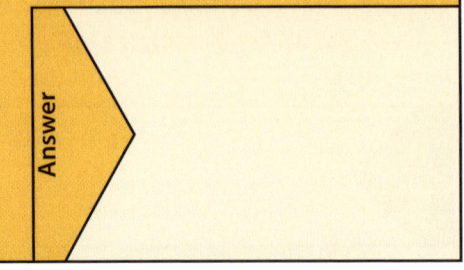

Answer:

Genetic Engineering

We can't control which genes an offspring will inherit, so selective breeding is a gradual process of trial and error. However, scientists can now 'engineer' organisms with specific genes by …

- identifying the gene that causes the required characteristic, for example, long stem, high milk yield;
- removing the required gene from one organism's DNA and putting it into another's.

GM crops are **g**enetically **m**odified in this way. And it's not just plants. Animals and micro-organisms can be modified too.

Did you know?

Killer cabbages: there's a type of genetically engineered cabbage that can kill caterpillars. The cabbages have been combined with a gene from a scorpion. They can now grow poison in their sap!

Medical treatments

Gene therapy

Possible cure for genetic diseases caused by a single faulty gene such as cystic fibrosis and haemophilia. A healthy version of the gene is inserted directly into cells affected by the disease.

Stem cells

Cells before their function has been determined.

Potentially, scientists may be able to grow particular types of cells and tissues to replace those missing, damaged or diseased (from things like strokes, burns, diabetes or Parkinson's).

In vitro fertilisation

Helps couples conceive who have not been able to by normal means. Eggs collected from the mother are mixed with the father's sperm in a laboratory dish. When embryos have formed, 2-3 are implanted into the mother's womb (2-3 embryos are implanted to increase the chance of one surviving).

Cloning

The copying of biological material.

Reproductive cloning copies the genetic information of a whole organism (for example *Dolly* the sheep).

DNA cloning inserts a gene of interest from one organism into another (for example pest resistant crops).

Embryo cloning creates an embryo to harvest stem cells from. (The embryo is destroyed before growing into a baby).

Genetic engineering example: using bacteria to produce human insulin

Diabetics need daily insulin injections. Human insulin is now made by genetically modified *Escherichia coli* (E. coli) bacteria. They have had the appropriate human gene added to their DNA.

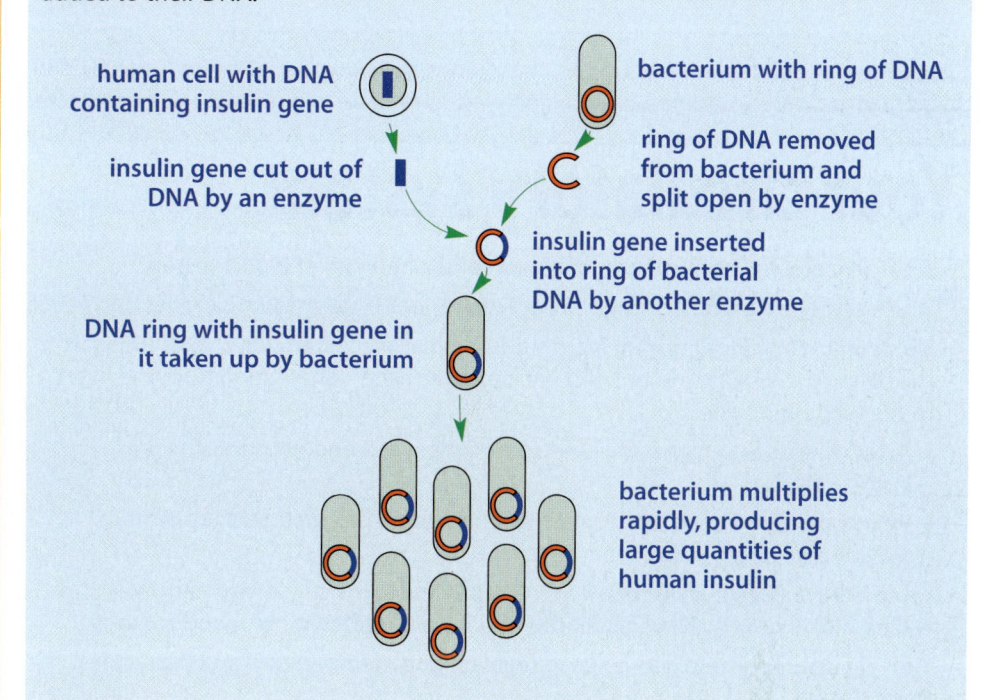

- human cell with DNA containing insulin gene
- insulin gene cut out of DNA by an enzyme
- bacterium with ring of DNA
- ring of DNA removed from bacterium and split open by enzyme
- insulin gene inserted into ring of bacterial DNA by another enzyme
- DNA ring with insulin gene in it taken up by bacterium
- bacterium multiplies rapidly, producing large quantities of human insulin

Other examples of genetic engineering

GM organism	Added gene	What it does
Pig	human gene	modifies pig's heart, making it appear human to a person's immune system. This avoids rejection when used for a human transplant.
Golden rice	vitamin A gene	produces rice containing vitamin A to help reduce blindness in malnourished children.
Tomato	fish 'anti-freeze' gene	makes tomatoes frost-resistant. The gene produces an anti-freeze chemical, which prevents the fish from freezing in cold water. Now it protects the tomatoes.

Evolutionary change

... is a change in the genetic make-up of a population during successive generations. It occurs because natural selection acts on genetic variations among individuals, which results in new species.

Environmental conditions can also affect evolutionary change. For example, the Ice age caused some species to die out.

Question 3
Genetic engineering uses enzymes.
When an organism is genetically modified, which three important stages involve enzymes?

Answer

77

Biological systems

Heart and lungs

The circulatory system consists of the heart, lungs and blood vessels and is involved in transporting blood around the body. Blood carries water, nutrients, oxygen and waste products to and from the body's cells.

Your circulatory system

- Your circulatory system consists of a heart and a network of blood vessels.
- Your heart is a muscle. It pumps blood around your body through arteries and veins.
- The human circulatory system is a double circulatory system. One takes blood from the heart to the body's organs and back, and the other takes blood from the heart to the lungs and back.
  - Arteries take blood from the heart, carrying oxygen and nutrients to your body's cells.
  - Veins take blood back to the heart, carrying waste products such as carbon dioxide away from cells.

  Arteries have thicker walls than veins. Arteries and veins divide into narrower, thin walled blood vessels called capillaries. You have 60,000 miles of blood vessels!
- Your circulatory system also helps to regulate body temperature and protect it from disease.

You have to imagine you're looking in a mirror when you look at the diagram (right):
- your right atrium and right ventricle appear on the left side of the diagram;
- your left atrium and left ventricle appear on the right side of the diagram.

Question 1
(a) Which blood vessels carry oxygenated blood and which carry deoxygenated blood?
(b) How do substances in the blood get into cells?
(c) Why do capillaries have thin walls?

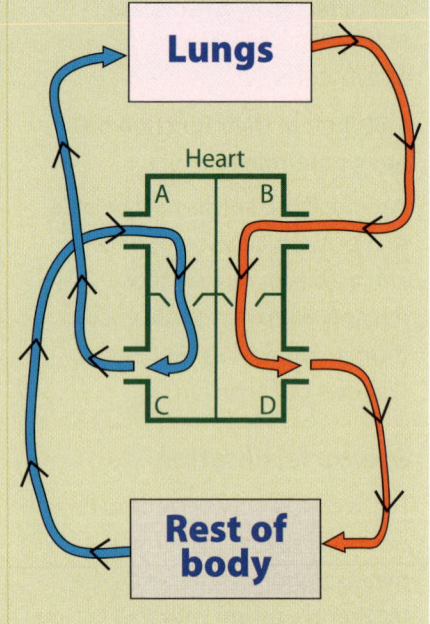

A = right atrium   B = left atrium
C = right ventricle   D = left ventricle
◆ = deoxygenated blood
◆ = oxygenated blood

Your heart

If you check the pulses of your friends and relatives, you will find that most hearts beat about 70 times a minute. The heart muscle is contracting and relaxing (a bit like clenching and unclenching a fist).

The top half of the heart has two atria (singular: atrium). These are chambers into which blood flows:
- oxygenated blood from the lungs into the left atrium
- deoxygenated blood from the body into the right atrium.

The bottom half has two ventricles. These are chambers which pump blood out:
- oxygenated blood to the body from the left ventricle
- deoxygenated blood to the lungs from the right ventricle.

Question 2
(a) How many times does blood pass through the heart during one circuit of the body?
(b) What stops blood from flowing in the wrong direction when the heart contracts?

Clues for crossword (right)...

Across:
1. These contract and force blood into the ventricles.
5. Blood vessels that carry blood away from the heart.
7. Tiny air sacs where gas diffusion takes place.
10. The trachea divides into two of these.
11. You find 7 across at the end of these.
12. It moves down when you breath in.

Down:
2. Windpipe.
3. The part of body containing the heart and lungs.
4. Blood is pumped out of one of these chambers in the heart.
6. One of the bones that makes up the cage that protects your lungs.
8. A blood vessel that carries blood to the heart.
9. It's pumped around the body by your heart.

78

Burning energy

The body's metabolic rate is the rate the body burns calories.

Even when asleep you're burning calories. This is your **basal metabolic rate**.

You burn additional calories when you're active and by the process of eating and digestion.

To maintain a stable weight you must take in the same number of calories as you burn.

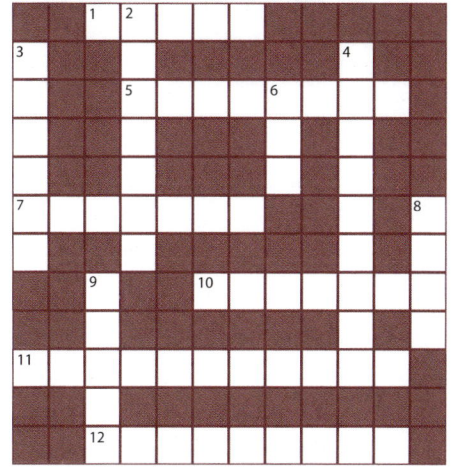

Your thorax

Your **thorax** is the part of your body that consists of your rib cage containing (and protecting) your heart and lungs.

Question 3
(a) Why does your body need oxygen? (b) Why does your body produce waste carbon dioxide?

Answer

Breathing or ventilation

When you breath in:
- diaphragm muscles and rib muscles **contract**;
- the diaphragm moves **down** and your ribs **rise**;
- the pressure **decreases** and air is **drawn into** your lungs;
- the volume of the thorax **increases**.

When you breath out:
- diaphragm muscles and rib muscles **relax**;
- the diaphragm moves **up** and your ribs **lower**;
- the pressure **increases** and air is **forced out** of your lungs;
- the volume of the thorax **decreases**.

When you breath in, air passes down the **trachea** (windpipe). At the entrance to the lungs the trachea goes into tubes called **bronchi** (singular **bronchus**). Each of these divides into smaller tubes called **bronchioles**. At the end of each of these are sets of air sacs called **alveoli**.

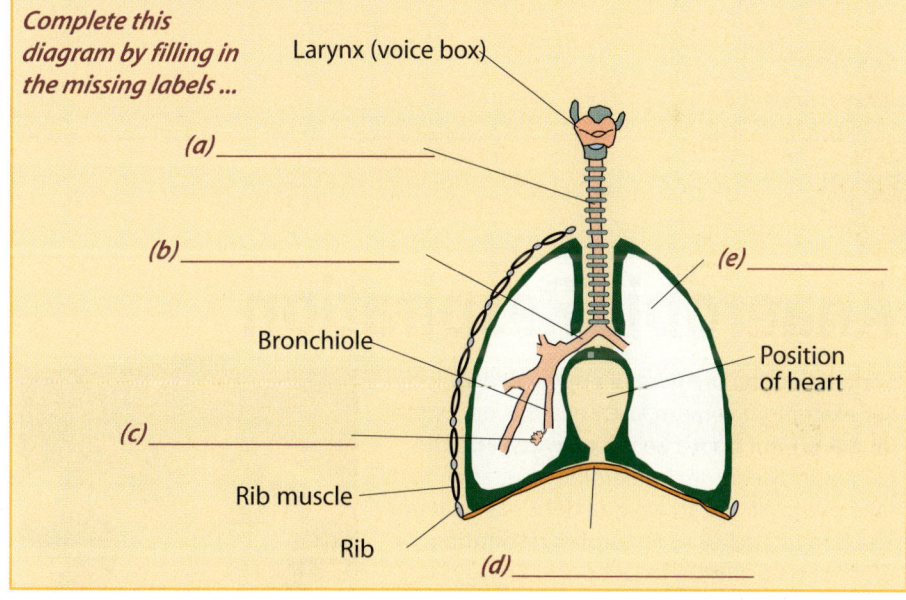

Complete this diagram by filling in the missing labels ...

- Larynx (voice box)
- (a) _____
- (b) _____
- Bronchiole
- (c) _____
- Rib muscle
- Rib
- (d) _____
- (e) _____
- Position of heart

Top tip: Think about what is happening as you breathe. This is a good way to deal with exam nerves, too.

Gas exchange

Alveoli are tiny - smaller than a grain of salt. There are 300 million in your lungs. Alveoli are covered with blood capillaries. This means there is a huge surface area through which gases can diffuse in and out of blood. The result is that gases can diffuse in and out of blood easily.

Question 4
Which are the main gases that diffuse through alveoli?

Answer

Biological systems

The body at work

Blood transports substances around the body and contains cells and molecules which protect the body from infection and disease. Blood transports all the substances that cells need to respire. Respiration is the chemical reaction that occurs in cells to produce energy. When there is sufficient oxygen, aerobic respiration occurs, but when there isn't, anaerobic respiration occurs.

Your blood and you

You have read how the heart pumps blood around your body. You've got about 5 dm^3 of it. Arteries carry food and oxygen to your body's cells. Veins carry waste products such as carbon dioxide away from cells. Antibodies are produced in the blood to fight disease. Blood is about 45% cells and 55% plasma.

What's in your blood?	What does it do?
Red blood cells • no nucleus.	Transport (carry) oxygen from the lungs to other parts of the body.
White blood cells • have a nucleus.	Part of your immune system; help to fight disease.
Plasma • a liquid.	Carries dissolved food and other substances to cells, and carries waste products away from cells (for example, carbon dioxide to the lungs).
Platelets • cell fragments.	Clump together to form a clot and stop bleeding after injury.

Question 1
What is anaemia?

Answer

Anaerobic Respiration

Sometimes you use a lot of energy very quickly. For example, if you run fast. Keep this up for too long and your body can't get oxygen into the cells quickly enough for aerobic respiration to take place. We say an **oxygen debt** has built up. The body switches to **anaerobic respiration**. Glucose is converted to lactic acid. Energy is released. But unlike aerobic respiration, no oxygen is used. The word equation is:

glucose → lactic acid + energy

Anaerobic respiration releases less energy than aerobic respiration. Also, lactic acid is toxic and, if it builds up, makes your legs heavy and your muscles ache. When a runner stops they take deep breaths and the body respires aerobically again.

Question 3
What happens to the lactic acid formed during anaerobic respiration?

Answer

Respiration

We all need energy. Even when you are sleeping your body uses energy. **Respiration** describes the energy released when certain chemical reactions take place in cells.

Remember: respiration is not the same as breathing.

Aerobic Respiration

Aerobic respiration is the process by which energy is released from food. The word equation is:

glucose + oxygen →
carbon dioxide + water + energy

It happens as long as there is enough oxygen. Most endurance work, for example, long walks and running long distances, is powered by aerobic respiration.

Question 2
How does your body supply cells with sufficient oxygen?

Answer

Protective mechanisms

Constant body temperature

Your body's temperature is usually about 37 °C. If it gets more than a couple of degrees higher or lower, you won't feel well.

So it's important your body maintains a constant temperature. There is a **thermoregulatory centre** in your brain. It monitors and controls body temperature. **Receptor cells** in your body sense temperature changes and send signals to your brain. They are sent via the **central nervous system**.

"I'm cold" signals trigger:
- your muscles to contract (you start shivering) and this releases heat energy
- capillaries in your skin to constrict (get smaller in diameter) so that blood flows more slowly.

"I'm hot" signals trigger:
- your sweat glands to release more sweat, cooling you down by evaporation
- capillaries in your skin to dilate (get bigger in diameter) so that blood can flow more quickly.

Glucose levels in the blood

Your body uses glucose to produce energy. The amount in your blood (the **glucose level** or **blood sugar level**) is monitored and controlled by cells in the pancreas.

Question 4
What's the process by which energy is released in cells?   > Answer

If your glucose level is high, for example after you have just eaten:
- your pancreas produces **insulin** (a hormone) which goes into the blood
- insulin helps your liver to remove glucose from your blood
- the glucose is changed into **glycogen** which is stored in the liver.

If your glucose level is low, for example after you have exercised:
- your pancreas releases **glucagon** (another hormone)
- glucagon triggers your liver to change glycogen back to glucose which goes into the blood.

Question 5
Two hormones control glucose levels in the blood. What are they?   > Answer

Adrenaline

Adrenaline is a hormone released by the body in situations of fear or stress. It results in increased:

- blood-sugar levels
- heart rate
- blood flow to muscles.

It also:

- reduces blood flow to the skin with the production of sweat
- widens the bronchioles in the lungs
- dilates the pupils.

All of these factors enable the body to respond more effectively.

So, athletes can compete, humans in danger can run away - and you can write quickly in your exams!

Senses, reflexes and reflex arcs

Humans have five senses: **touch, taste, sight, hearing, smell**.

Your body uses a reflex arc when immediate action is needed. A protective response is generated directly from the spinal cord without requiring the brain to process information. In the example below:

1. hand touches Bunsen flame; **2.** touch sensors detect heat; **3.** message travels along sensory neurons to the spinal cord; **4.** relay neurones passes the message to a motor neurone; **5.** arm muscle contracts moving the hand away.

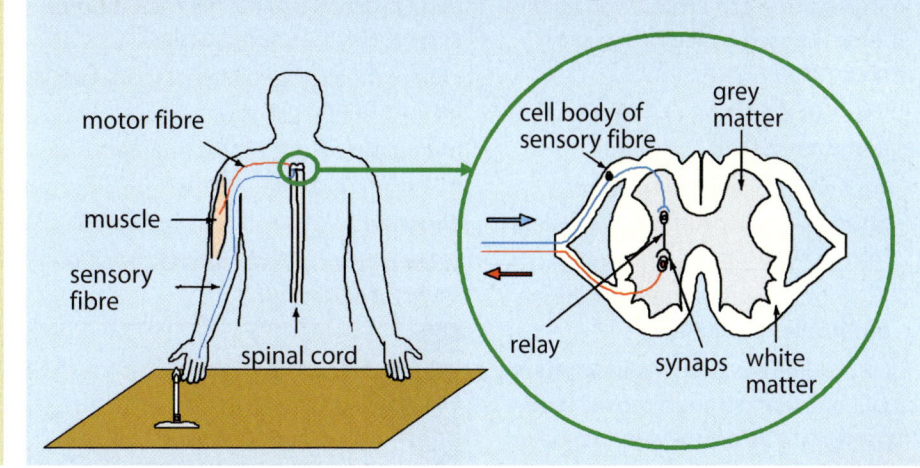

81

Biological systems

Micro-organisms and disease

Some diseases and illnesses are caused by micro-organisms. It's the job of the immune system to fight off these infections. Antibiotics can be given to someone to help them fight off certain types of bacterial infections. Immunisation prepares the immune system to be able to fight off infection from a particular type of micro-organism. It can work against viral or bacterial infections.

Micro-organisms and disease

Bacteria
Most are harmless: millions live on your skin and inside your body.
Some are essential: for example, they are needed for digestion.

Pathogens
Some micro-organisms are harmful: they cause disease and are commonly called 'germs'.
There are three types: **fungi, bacteria** and **viruses**.

Here are some examples of pathogens.
Test your memory by covering up the symptoms column ...

Type of pathogen	Example of a disease it causes	Symptoms (effects)
Fungi	athlete's foot	flaking skin between the toes
Bacteria	tuberculosis (TB)	lung inflammation, spreading to other organs
	skin infections (e.g. impetigo) caused by *Staphylococcus aureus*	boils and pimples containing pus
Viruses	measles	severe rash of pink spots spreading across the body
	mumps	painful swelling of glands beside the ears
	rubella	rash similar to measles, but less severe
	polio	fever, headache and stiffness (in severe cases, muscles become paralysed)
	foot and mouth (in sheep and cattle)	blisters on the feet and in the mouth

Protection by immunisation

Immunisation can protect you against diseases caused by harmful micro-organisms.

- Vaccines work by kick-starting your **immune** system.
- Your white blood cells recognise **antigens** on the surface of invading micro-organisms.
- So, your immune system produces **antibodies** to kill them.

Most children are given MMR vaccine at about one year old and a second dose (booster) just before they start school.

MMR protects against measles, mumps and rubella (German measles).
You might also have been vaccinated against TB and polio.
Immunisation only helps prevent disease. It does not cure it.

Question 1
What disease can sheep and cattle be immunised against?

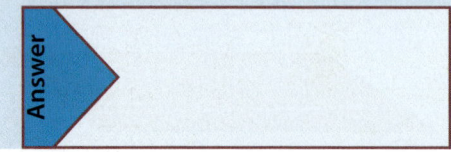

Answer

Coughs and sneezes spread diseases

Harmful micro-organisms must get inside your body to cause illness.
Diseases spread:
- by breathing in contaminated dust and water droplets (for example, influenza, measles, TB)
- through contaminated food and water (for example, salmonella, cholera, polio, dysentery)
- through cuts, scratches and bites (for example, malaria, hepatitis B, MRSA, tetanus).

Question 2
How do coughs and sneezes spread diseases?

Answer

Vaccines, vaccinations and immunisation

- **Vaccines** are used to protect the body against harmful micro-organisms.
- **Vaccination** is how you are given the vaccine (for example, by injection or by mouth).
- **Immunisation** means helping your immune system protect your body against infections.

Complete this sentence:

Doctors vaccinate with _____
to boost the _____ system
against _____ caused by
harmful _____.

82

Auto-immune diseases

Auto-immune diseases are caused by the immune system malfunctioning and attacking part of its own body. For example:

Multiple sclerosis

Immune system attacks myelin sheaths which insulate and protect nerve cells (a bit like the coverings on electrical wires do).

Destroying myelin prevents the brain communicating with the rest of the body correctly. So muscles become weak, can tingle and cause unsteadiness. There are many other symptoms too.

Rheumatoid arthritis

Caused by the immune system attacking the tissue surrounding joints called synovium. Joints become inflamed and painful. Eventually the inflammation damages the joint.

Crohn's disease

Inflammation of the digestive tract, most commonly the ileum (lower small intestine). It might be caused by the immune system attacking food, bacteria and other substances in the intestine. White blood cells accumulate in the lining of the intestine causing inflammation leading to ulcers and bowel injury.

Use and misuse of drugs

Drugs affect health. Drugs such as medicinhes can help people if they are used correctly.

Sometimes, people choose to take drugs for social reasons.

Drugs such as cannabis, nicotine, alcohol, solvents, heroin and caffeine can have harmful effects.

Some are legal, such as nicotine and caffeine. Some are illegal, such as cannabis and heroin. Some are not intended to be used as drugs, such as solvents (glue sniffing).

Antibiotics

If you get an infection, your doctor may prescribe an **antibiotic**.

There are two types:
- Antibiotics that kill bacteria are called **bactericidal**. Penicillin is an example.
- Antibiotics that stop bacteria multiplying are called **bacteriostatic** (static means 'not moving').

Antibiotics can't kill viruses or stop them multiplying. Sometimes the bacteria which attack your immune system can become resistant to antibiotics, so they need to be used carefully. As with all medicines, there can be side-effects: the most common are diarrhoea, feeling sick and being sick.

Question 3
What's a **child immunisation schedule**?

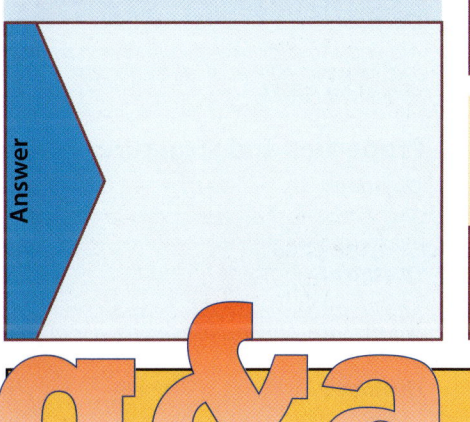

Answer

Wanted: dead or alive

Even dead micro-organisms have antigens. If you put dead micro-organisms into your body it produces antibodies. The antibodies then lie in wait for an invasion.

As soon as harmful micro-organisms appear, the antibodies kill them.

The typhoid vaccine is an example.

Live, weak, harmful micro-organisms can work in the same way. The MMR vaccine is one example.

Question 4
Man has always suffered from diseases, but their causes have only been discovered in the last two hundred years. Suggest why.

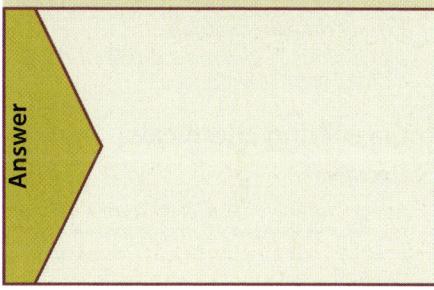

Answer

Question 5
Name two human diseases due to a virus that cause a body rash.

Answer

q & a

Q. How do micro-organisms cause disease?

A. They multiply inside cells. As a result:
- cells can't work normally, so that part of the body doesn't work properly
- cells may be destroyed;
- these pathogens may release toxins (poisons) into the bloodstream, and so affect other parts of the body.

Q. My doctor says antibiotics won't cure my cold, because it's caused by a virus, not bacteria. What's the difference?

A. Viruses ...
- are much smaller than bacteria - visible only with electron microscopes
- have no cells, cytoplasm or nucleus - just a DNA chain inside a protein *packet*
- can't reproduce themselves - they invade cells, which then copy the viral DNA
- are not affected by antibiotics - they don't have the parts that antibiotics attack.

Q. What's the difference between infectious diseases and contagious diseases?

A. Infectious diseases are passed from one person to another.

Contagious diseases spread by touch. It needn't be direct touch between two people. The harmful micro-organisms can also be passed via surfaces such as door handles or taps.

Q. What's an epidemic?

A. It's when a disease spreads rapidly and lots of people come down with the same illness.

83

Answers to questions

Raw materials

Fill in the missing word ...
Liquid.

Question 1
Impurities don't matter. Bits of dirt and grit help tyres to grip the icy surface. It's cheaper than pure salt.

Question 2
It saves energy, so reduces costs.

Question 3
(a) Compounds made up of only hydrogen and carbon, like methane, CH_4 and octane, C_8H_{18}
(b) Gasoline.
(c) Check your answer against the diagram.
(d) Gas oil.

Question 4
Hydrogen.

Question 5
By evaporation of water.

Extract the raw materials ...
1. Limestone 2. Rock salt 3. Crude oil 4. Sulfur 5. Metal ores 5. Marble

Classifying chemicals

Question 1
(a) sodium & bromine (b) calcium & fluorine (c) silicon & oxygen (d) phosphorus & chlorine Ee) silver, nitrogen & oxygen (f) lead, sulfur & oxygen.

Question 2
A, C, D

Names and formulae ...
ammonia, carbon dioxide, water, hydrochloric acid, sulfuric acid, calcium oxide, iron oxide, lead oxide, sodium hydroxide, barium chloride, sodium chloride, calcium carbonate, copper carbonate, sodium carbonate, potassium nitrate, silver nitrate, barium sulfate, copper sulfate, sodium sulfate, methane.

Question 3
(a) bulk inorganic (b) fine organic (c) fine inorganic (d) fine inorganic (e) bulk organic (f) fine organic.

Atomic structure

Question 1
A vacuum.

Question 2
electrons = negative, protons = positive.

Question 3
(a) 6 (b) 17 (c) Nitrogen (N).

Question 4
(a) lithium; sodium; potassium; rubidium; caesium.
(b) sodium; magnesium; aluminium; silicon; phosphorus; sulfur; chlorine; argon.

Complete this table ...
(a) 9 (b) 19 (c) 11 (d) 11 (e) 29 (f) 29 (g) 63 (h) 82 (i) 125 (j) 82.

Complete these six facts ...
(a) protons (b) electrons (c) atomic mass (d) neutrons (e) mass (f) relative.

Chemical bonding

Question 1
(a) 2.7 (b) 2.8.3 (c) 2.8.6

Question 2
A metal ion has fewer electrons(-) than protons(+), so an overall positive charge. (1+ for each electron lost.)

Question 3
(a) (i) K^+ 2.8.8 (ii) S^{2-} 2.8.8
(b) K_2S.

Question 4
(i) covalent (ii) ionic (iii) covalent.

Question 5
$Cl_2 + 2Br^- \rightarrow 2Cl^- + Br_2$

Comparing materials

Question 1
(a) They react easily with air and water, so would corrode away too easily. (b) Chromium.

Question 2
(a) Answers could include poly(propene), polyurethane, polycarbonate, and PTFE (Teflon). (b) Poly means 'many'. Polymers have many 'monomer' units joined to form a chain.

Question 3
By heating to a very high temperature in a kiln to drive off all the water.

Question 4
Answers could include carbon fibre in fishing rods, or wood fibre in medium density fibreboard (MDF).

Properties and structure

Question 1
They have only 1 outer electron, so the 'sea' has fewer electrons to hold the ions.

Question 2
(a) Zinc (b) Less malleable, because zinc atoms make it more difficult for layers of atoms to slide.

Question 3
The fitting will get hot from the lamp. A thermoset will not soften or melt because of cross-links between the polymer molecules. The wiring needs to be flexible. Plasticiser allows pvc molecules to move past each other.

Question 4
Covalent.

Wordsearch pairs ...
(1) Lead and tin. (2) Copper and zinc.

Formulae and equations

Question 1
(a) copper, sulfate and oxygen (1:1:4)
(b)(i) potassium chloride (ii) lead sulfate (iii) magnesium carbonate (iv) sulfur dioxide.

Question 2
(a) CH_4 (b) O_2 (c) CO_2 (d) H_2O

Question 3
nitrogen + hydrogen $\rightarrow$ ammonia
$N_2 + 3H_2 \rightarrow 2NH_3$

Reacting masses

Question 1
$12 + 1 + (3 \times 35.5) = 119.5$

Question 2
(a) 48 g (b) 5.6 g (c) 22 g

Question 3
(a) $12 + (4 \times 1) = 16$ grams
(b) $6.02 \times 10^{23} \times 0.001 = 6.02 \times 10^{20}$

Question 4
(a) 0.1 (b) 0.5 (c) 0.15

Question 5
(a) 22 g CO_2 (b) 18 g H_2O

Complete this list ...
metre; second; gram; kelvin; ampere.

Chemical change

Question 1
(a) the reaction is exothermic (b) the reaction is endothermic.

Question 1
(a) 40°C (b) 105 Pa (c) 2 mol dm^{-3} (d) aluminium powder.

Getting metals from ores

Question 1
(a) An ore is a mineral from which a metal is extracted (b) iron ore = haematite or magnetite; lead ore = galena or cerrusite. (There are others, but these are the main ores).

Question 2
A combination of metals with its own special properties.

Question 3
(a) calcium carbonate (b) By using the hot waste gases from the top of the furnace. (c) Nitrogen (air with its oxygen used up) and carbon dioxide.

Label the diagram ...
(a) Raw materials (b) Hot waste gases (c) Hot air blast (d) Iron (e) Slag.

Names of the chemicals ...
lead oxide + carbon monoxide $\rightarrow$ lead + carbon dioxide.

Question 4
It is oxidised to sulfur dioxide, SO_2

Question 5
(a) (i) $Na^+ + e^- \rightarrow Na$ (ii) $2Cl^- \rightarrow Cl_2 + 2e^-$
(b) $2NaCl \rightarrow 2Na + Cl_2$

Organic compounds

Question 1

(a)
```
    H   H
    |   |
H - C - C - H
    |   |
    H   H
```

(b)
```
    H   H   H
    |   |   |
H - C - C - C - H
    |   |   |
    H   H   H
```

(c)

H H H H
| | | |
H—C—C—C—C—H
| | | |
H H H H

Question 2
(a) three hydrogen atoms and one carbon atom (b) two hydrogen atoms and two carbon atoms.

Question 3
C_nH_{2n}

Question 4
Ethane, ethene and hydrogen.

Conservation of energy

Question 1
Chemical energy.

Question 2
(a) chemical (b) potential (c) chemical (d) kinetic.

Complete the energy transfer diagram ...
A = electrical; B = sound

Question 3
(a) Light energy and heat energy (b) Light, sound and a little heat.

Question 4
(a) 500,000 joules (b) 300,000 joules.

Wordsearch law ...
Energy cannot be created or destroyed.

Energy loss and heat transfer

Question 1
The sum of all the forms of energy that are produced.

Question 2
100 %

Question 3
(a) 1220 joules (b) Heat energy.
(c) efficiency = (780 x 100)/2000 = 39%

Wordsearch formulae ...
efficiency = useful energy x 100 / input energy

waste energy = useful energy - output energy

Conduction, convection and radiation

Question 1
An insulator.

Question 2
Because it reflects radiant heat from the radiator back into a room.

Question 3
Conduction.

Question 4
(a) Convection (b) Radiation (c) Conduction.

Question 5
(a) Conduction and convection. (b) Conduction through the tank walls, then radiation and convection.

Question 6
Shiny.

Wordsearch pairs

2 with 3. 4 with 6. 5 with 1

Fossil fuels

Question 1
They will not last forever and cannot be replaced.

Question 2
Carbon and hydrogen.

Question 3
Coal is solid. Oil is liquid.

Question 4
Because they are made of carbon compounds.

Question 5
(1) Non-renewable (or finite). (2) Carbon dioxide formed which could cause global warming. (3) Sulfur dioxide pollutes the air.

Alternative energy resources

Question 1
Splitting into smaller pieces.

Fill in the gaps ...
A energy B combustion (burning) C finite or non-renewable D radiation (or radioactive emissions) E complicated (or difficult) F explosion G waste.

Question 2
We never produce it; we change it from one form to another.

Question 3
Where the wind's energy is harvested.

Question 4
The home of a living organism.

Generating electricity

Question 1
fossil fuel + oxygen → carbon dioxide + water

Question 2
(a) chemical (b) kinetic.

Question 3
(a) It escapes into the atmosphere (b) Law of conservation of energy.

Question 4
Energy demands are greater in winter, when it's cold and dark, than in summer.

Choosing and using energy resources

Question 1
(a) oil or coal (b) wood.

Question 2
6.5/1.7 = 3.82

Question 3
(a) (i) Button. (ii) Button. (iii) Rechargeable. (iv) Conventional or rechargeable.
(b) (i) 4 (ii) 6

Question 4
Electric hotplate

Question 4
Environmental scientists, geoscientists, meteorologists, scientists studying traffic flow.

Counting the cost

Question 1
Conduction, convection and radiation.

Question 2
A liquid transfers the heat energy faster because its particles are closer together.

Unscramble the letters ...
(good ...) aluminium, copper, graphite, iron, steel.

(not good ...) cardboard, ceramic, plastic, rubber, wood.

Complete the labels ...
A turbine B generator C power cables taking electricity to the National Grid D heat exchanger.

Question 3
Heat energy is transferred from the vapour to a coolant (usually water) and the liquid condenses.

Question 4
(a) 50 x 4.18 x 5 = 1045 joules (b) 100 x 2.42 x 5 = 1210 joules.

Useful products from living organisms

Question 1
leather, penicillin, wool.

Question 2
Cotton.

Ecosystems

Question 1
three.

Question 2
Pyramid of number: Ad = easy to get values; Disad = size not considered at each trophic level.

Pyramid of energy: Ad = most accurate representation of feeding relationships; Disad = harder to take measurements, and have to take them over long period.

Pyramid of biomass: Ad = accounts for size and amount of organisms at each trophic level; Disad = have to kill the organism to get the value.

Match the terms ...
Producer = Produces its own food by photosynthesis.

Consumer = Consumes other organisms for food.

Omnivore = Eats plants and animals.

Herbivore = Eats only plants.

Carnivore = Eats only other animals.

Decomposer = Bacteria or fungi. Feed on decaying matter.

Trophic level = Level in a food chain dependent on the method of feeding. All organisms in the same trophic level of a food web are the same number of energy transfers away from the producer of energy.

85

Farming

Question 1
N = Nitrogen P = Phosphorus K = Potassium.

Question 2
(a) Crop yield will not increase any further. Plants cannot use more than they need. (b) Unused fertiliser is washed into lakes & rivers causing eutrophication.

Question 3
Manure from the animals puts nutrients into the soil to replace those taken out by crops.

How organisms grow

Question 1
Oxygen gas ($6O_2$).

Question 2
(a) Catalyst (b) Endothermic, since it needs to take in energy to keep going.

Question 3
In: sunlight, carbon dioxide, water. *Out:* oxygen, glucose.

Question 4
(a) Faster rate of photosynthesis, so faster growth; (b) Higher CO_2 level and temperature, so even faster growt; (c) Plants photosynthese for longer each day, so more growth.

Crossword
Across: 1. mitosis; 2. genetics; 3. pituitary
Down: 1. nitrates; 2. fertilisation; 3. cancer; 4. meiosis; 5. puberty.

Micro-organisms

Question 1
(a) Micro-organisms reproduce too slowly, or not at all. (b) Enzymes are 'denatured' - their structure is altered so they can no longer catalyse the reactions. The micro-organisms may be killed.

Unscramble the words …
(a) antibiotics (b) bacteria.

Complete the paragraph …
Words in correct order: milk • bacteria • lactose • lactic acid • acidity • casein • coagulate.

Question 2
(a) Hands and face; plastic equipment that would melt or deform at high temperatures. (b) Because harmful bacteria spread much more quickly from wet hands than dry hands.

Cells and their contents

Question 1
Red blood cells.

Question 2
mitochondria.

Question 3
Photosynthesis takes place in chloroplasts. Animals don't make their own food by photosynthesis. They feed by eating plants and/or other animals.

Question 4
(a) C, H and O (b) C, H, O and N.

Question 5
(a) CO_2 in, O_2 out (b) O_2 in, CO_2 out.

Wordsearch highlights …
cell wall, vacuole, chloroplast.

How cells divide

Question 1
(a) pollen [male] and egg / ovule [female].
(b) sperm [male] and egg / ovum [female].

Question 2
Mutation.

Question 3
(i) A child is conceived when gametes from each parent fuse to make a new cell, from which the child develops. Half of the cell's genetic material (DNA) comes from each parent.
(ii) During meiosis, chromosome pairs exchange some of their genes. So, each gamete contains a random combination of genes. New cells formed by fertilisation are therefore different each time.

Passing on genes

Question 1
(a) Gametes. They contain half as many chromosomes as normal cells (b) Any features common to all humans, e.g. 2 arms/legs, 5 fingers/toes, upright stance (c) Specific differences, e.g. colour of skin / hair / eyes, facial appearance.

Question 2
Hh = dominant / heterozygous; hH = dominant / heterozygous; hh = recessive / homozygous.

Complete the example …
Chance of blue eyes is 2 in 4 (50%).

Question 3
None, since all offspring will inherit the dominant B from their father, giving them brown eyes.

Controlling gene inheritance

Question 1
Allow onion plants to flower. Pollinate flowers of the largest onions with pollen from other large ones. Collect and grow the resulting seeds. Repeat this process many times.

Question 2
(b) and (d) are impossible, because the two parents are from different genus (i.e. unrelated).

Question 3
(i) removing the required gene from the original DNA chain.
(ii) cutting open the DNA of the organism to be modified.
(iii) inserting the new gene into the gap in the DNA.

Heart and lungs

Question 1
(a) Oxygenated blood - arteries, deoxygenated blood - veins (exceptions are the pulmonary arteries and pulmonary veins) (b) By diffusion (c) Diffusion occurs more quickly through thin walls.

Question 2
(a) Twice (b) One-way valves.

Question 3
(a) It's used to release energy in cells by reacting with glucose (b) It's a product of the reaction between oxygen and glucose in cells.

Complete the diagram …
(a) trachea (b) bronchus (c) alveolus (d) diaphragm (e) lung.

Question 4
Oxygen and carbon dioxide.

The body at work

Question 1
Anaemia means insufficient red blood cells to carry the amount of oxygen your body needs.

Question 2
When you breath, air gets into your lungs. Oxygen in this air diffuses into your blood and is carried by red blood cells to where it's needed.

Question 3
When oxygen is available again, the toxic lactic acid is broken down.

Question 4
Respiration.

Question 5
Insulin and glucagon.

Micro-organisms and disease

Question 1
Foot and mouth, caused by a virus.

Question 2
Micro-organisms in water droplets spread and infect people nearby.

Complete the sentence …
Doctors vaccinate with vaccines to boost the immune system against diseases caused by harmful micro-organisms.

Question 3
It's a series of vaccinations during a child's life to protect them against the more common diseases. Parents are given the choice to have their children immunised or not.

Question 4
The micro-organisms that cause disease are so small they could not be seen until powerful microscopes were developed.

Question 5
Measles and rubella (German measles).